Perfect Clarity

Perfect Clarity

A Tibetan Buddhist Anthology of Mahamudra and Dzogchen

Writings by

Padmashambhava, Yeshe Tsogyal, Longchenpa,
Milarepa, Tulku Urgyen Rinpoche, and others

Translated by
Erik Pema Kunsang

Compiled by
Marcia Schmidt

Edited by
Marcia Schmidt and Michael Tweed

Rangjung Yeshe Publications
Flat 5a, Greenview Garden
125 Robinson Road, Hong Kong
www.rangjung.com

Copyright © 2012 Rangjung Yeshe Publications

Address letters to:
Rangjung Yeshe Publications
Box 1200, Kathmandu, Nepal

1 2 3 4 5 6 7 8 9

First Paperback Edition 2012

Publication Data:
Perfect Clarity: A Tibetan Buddhist Anthology of
Mahamudra and Dzogchen.
Translated by Erik Pema Kunsang (Erik Hein Schmidt).
Compiled and Edited by Marcia B. Schmidt with Michael Tweed.

ISBN 978–962–7341–697 (pbk.)

Eastern Philosophy—Buddhism. 2. Buddhism—Doctrines.
3. Vajrayana—Tibet.

Cover Design: Maryann Lipaj
Cover Photo: Courtesy of Mani Lama

Mahamudra and dzogchen
Differ in words but not in meaning.
The only difference is that mahamudra stresses mindfulness,
While dzogchen relaxes within awareness.

—Tsele Natsok Rangdrol

Contents

Unity

PREFACE

Marcia Binder Schmidt

For practitioners on the paths of dzogchen and mahamudra, one of the greatest joys is to personally receive oral instructions from a realized teacher. The excitement of being able to train based on that advice is further enhanced by the stimulation and support that guidance manuals provide. The pith teachings contained in these texts are so simple and direct that once we have received personal instructions, we can easily apply them without fear of mistakes. All of the selections presented in this book offer incredible knowledge that is inspiring and vital.

In collecting these pieces, I sensed the irony that even though most of these masters were the greatest scholars of their time, they were also renowned for their spiritual accomplishment, and although erudite, they wrote pithy, practical advice as well. Drawing on their combined learning and accomplishment, the likes of Gampopa, Longchenpa, and Jamgon Kongtrul—to mention just a few—composed user-friendly guidance manuals distilling and refining the instructions to their quintessential points. For us ordinary beings, these essential, condensed points need to once again be unpacked by our teacher's instructions. It is never enough to merely read texts like this and think that we can totally understand them without relying on a master's explanation. Even though full comprehension and assimilation results from practice, we need to be nurtured and guided. Only then are the three perfect measures complete, namely, taking the support of the words of the Buddha and realized masters, taking the support of our teacher's oral instructions, and taking the support of our own pure experience and intelligence.

Perfect Clarity begins with supplications that are intended as a prelude to the book, as well as prayers for practitioners to use when meditating at home. Next are teachings presented from the mahamudra perspective, followed by those of the dzogchen viewpont. The unity section combines both the mahamudra and dzogchen approaches. To be able to offer this anthology is the result of the work of many dedicated people. Sincere thanks go to the translator, Erik Pema Kunsang, who makes these pith instructions come alive; to his primary editor, Michael Tweed, who works tirelessly on language and connotation; to Meghan Howard, a most trusted and gifted copy editor who does not let the meaning slip away; to Dr. Lynn Schroeder and Michael Yockey, the constant and careful proofreaders; to Joan Olson, whose elegance in design is uplifting; and to Maryann Lipaj, the artist who creates inspirational covers.

As usual sincere expressions of gratitude go to Richard Gere and Mollie Rodriguez of the Gere Foundation for their continual support and belief in our work. In these difficult times such generosity for production and translation offers light on the treacherous path of originality and tradition combined.

In the end the most sincere appreciation goes to the various authors, the realized beings who never give up on us hopeless beings and who offer us guidance on every aspect of the path. May we somehow repay a fraction of their kindness by accomplishing the advice herein, producing unexcelled benefit for countless other lost sentient beings.

When taking this picture of Tulku Urgyen Rinpoche,
Erik requested a photograph that upon being seen would result
in a special connection with the dzogchen teachings.
Rinpoche replied, "Like this?"
Click!

AN INTRODUCTION
TO GUIDANCE MANUALS

Tulku Urgyen Rinpoche

Apply the three degrees of knowledge resulting from study, reflection, and meditation practice, as well as your theoretical understanding, experience, and realization, to the mahamudra and dzogchen teachings and you will possess everything necessary to reach the state of complete enlightenment in this very life.

In this dark age, the most effective style of teaching is not lengthy scholarly explanations but rather direct guidance manuals (*triyig*). The dzogchen tantras themselves were written in a style that shrouds and conceals the meaning so that only a master who is extremely well versed in oral instructions and treatises is able to clarify the meaning. On the other hand, based upon oral instructions, a guidance manual is a short, comprehensive teaching, written in a clear and simple manner. Such summaries of the mahamudra and dzogchen teachings contain all the teachings that a worthy practitioner requires to reach the state of primordial enlightenment in this very life.

Although mahamudra and dzogchen use different terminology, in actuality, their ultimate meanings do not differ at all. Through such teachings, at the time of death, the mind merges with dharmakaya the instant that its link to the physical body is severed. However, it is also possible to attain true and complete enlightenment in the dharmadhatu realm of Akanishtha while still remaining in this physical body.

Great teachers have said, recognition of rigpa occurs through gathering the accumulations and purifying obscurations, and through the blessings of a qualified master. Depending on other means should be known as delusion. Have you heard of anyone who recognized nondual awareness simply by reading books? Aside from receiving blessings, gathering the accumulations, and purifying obscurations, no other technique exists for recognizing rigpa.

Devotion is more important than scholarship. One could possibly gain impressive skill in debate and in analytical thought yet still find fault in the dzogchen teachings, believing them to be the erroneous view of followers of Hashang's school of Sudden Illumination.

Receiving blessings refers to a moment of deep devotion. Recognizing rigpa through mere intellectual speculation is indeed very difficult. The Kagyü and Nyingma schools emphasize the simple resting meditation of a kusulu as opposed to the analytical meditation of a pandita. Through the single method of devotion, receiving the blessings, and focusing on meditation, countless practitioners of the past have reached accomplishment.

The Kagyü and Nyingma are known more for a long line of realized masters than for great scholars. Although there have been several learned masters, for the most part, Kagyü and Nyingma followers have been male and female lay practitioners. The fact that countless numbers of these practitioners died while sitting up in undistracted wakefulness is due to this tradition of simple, direct teachings. You can read about this yourself in the wondrous histories of the followers of the Nyingma school, as well as of the various Kagyü lineages. However, one example is the siddha Seltong Shogom, who, together with a gathering of his disciples, left more than thirty clear footprints in solid rock. When I was young, my father took me to see these footprints in Eastern Tibet. In several places the rock had been molded like dough. Amazing!

On the fifteenth day of the lunar month, the full moon sets simultaneously with the sun's rising—there is no gap between these two events. Having full wing power at birth, a garuda can fly immediately upon hatching from its egg. Similarly, a dzogchen or mahamudra practitioner attains complete enlightenment concurrently with the death of the physical body. Hence, at the moment of death, an experienced yogi does not lose consciousness but reaches enlightenment!

SUPPLICATIONS

Longchenpa

CLOUD BANKS OF NECTAR

**A Yearning Supplication and Aspiration
to the Three Roots**

Longchenpa

Victorious ones and your children in the ten directions,
All assemblies of noble shravakas and pratyekabuddhas,
And everyone who practices the Dharma, I supplicate
  you respectfully.
Regard me with compassion and grant your blessings.

Gurus of the three lineages, peaceful and wrathful
  yidam deities,
Dakas and dakinis, buddhas and bodhisattvas,
Dharma protectors and samaya holders, rishis who have
  attained true speech,
Lovingly bestow your blessings on this supplicating child.

Kyema kyihu! A poor wretch like me

Has been tormented by unbearable karma and the three
    poisons for so long.
Stretch out your hands with great love and compassion
And guide me this very moment.

Although my nature is primordially enlightened,
Because of ignorance and confusion I have wandered
    throughout existence.
I am desolate in this dreamlike samsara.
Please be my refuge and protect me.

Please rescue me and countless sentient beings
From the endless ocean of samsara, so difficult to cross.
Take us across the sea of suffering
In the unsurpassable boat of wisdom.

The manifestations of long-ingrained habitual
    tendencies
And dualistic grasping to deluded experience are more
    imposing than Mount Sumeru.
Please demolish them this very moment
With the wisdom vajra of supreme liberation.

The darkness of ignorance, such a dense obscuration,
    has lasted so long;
It is hard to fathom and its end is impossible to see.
With your wisdom light rays, please clear away
This immense veil, which obscures the luminous
    essence.

All that I do is but the cause of afflictions and suffering.
Letting my mind turn completely away
From the futile concerns of this world,
Please make me spend day and night in Dharma
practice.

Incorrect thinking is like overlapping waves.
Various conceptualizations chase after the five sense
objects.
Please pacify the eight collections, the tendencies, and
the all-ground
Within dharmadhatu.

Conceptual tendencies, the afflicted mind of the desire
realm,
And habitual tendencies connected with the samsaric
mind
Of the clarity of the form realm and the nonthought of
the formless—
Please purify them all.

Having turned away from the pursuit of solitary peace,
The inferior attitude of practicing for the benefit of
oneself,
Let me enter the path of the supreme outer, inner, and
secret teachings,
And enable me to act vastly for the benefit of others.

Completely purifying the karma, the three poisons, and
    tendencies
Of all beings who are on an inferior, perverted, or
    mistaken path,
Please help everyone, without exception, to journey
    together
To the liberated citadel of the wish-fulfilling mind-
    essence.

We have remained for so long, without beginning or
    end
In the ocean of obscurations, murky with emotions,
With no chance for emancipation by ourselves.
Please liberate us with your great compassion.

From the strong and intense emotions, so hard to
    endure,
From the pain of existence with so much suffering,
And from the level of carelessness, dependency, and
    laziness,
Please fully liberate us this very day.

May we fully realize that all futile phenomena
Are impermanent, unstable, a magical enticement for
    the mind.
Please enable us to spend day and night continuously
With sincere renunciation and weariness.

Having attained awareness, superknowledge, and
    samadhi
In the delightful seclusion of sacred mountain
    dwellings,
Please enable us to arrive, within this very lifetime,
At the celestial realm of great bliss, the spontaneous
    accomplishment of the two benefits.

Exerting ourselves in practice, alone and with
    perseverance,
May we not drift toward the concerns of this life for an
    instant.
Perfecting the siddhis in the footsteps of the forefathers,
May we always please our spiritual master.

Free from the flaws of broken samayas
And unmistakenly realizing the meaning of the view,
    meditation, action, and result,
Without wavering from the luminous state, day or
    night,
May we accomplish the twofold benefit for self and
    others.

Perfecting development and completion, the purity of
    what appears and exists,
Let the ocean of dakinis and samaya holders gather like
    cloud banks.
With the twofold siddhis descending on us like rain,
May we accomplish the four activities.

With pure perception and devotion arising without bias,
With uninterrupted love and compassion,
And with experience and realization—the virtues of
    view and meditation—blazing forth,
May we impartially act for the welfare of all beings.

Through this, our perfect devotion and merit,
May all beings be fully liberated together, without
    exception,
And journey within this very lifetime
To Samantabhadra's realm of spontaneously present
    great bliss.

This supplication was made at Lharing Drag, the seat of the Self-Born Padma, by Longchen Rabjam, a yogi of the Supreme Vehicle who has attained unshakable faith in all the holy masters and is rich with the wealth of learning. May this be auspicious throughout all directions and times.

Samantrabhadra

The Cloud Bank
of Blessings

A Supplication to the Ocean of the Three Roots
and the Dharma Protectors

Jamyang Khyentse Wangpo

Namo guru dheva dakini ganebhyah

Samantabhadra, Vajradhara, and the five aspects of
Immense Ocean,[1]
Greatly renowned twelve illustrious teachers,[2]
Holders of the buddhas' mind transmission filling all
of space,
I supplicate you; bestow your blessings and siddhis.

Lord of Secrets, Garab Dorje, Manjushrimitra, and
Shri Singha,

---

1. The buddhas of the five families.
2. The twelve buddhas of the Good Aeon.

Jnanasutra, and twenty-one panditas,
Mind, space, and instruction masters of the symbolic
    transmission,
I supplicate you; bestow your blessings and siddhis.

Three family sattvas, five noble disciples,
King Jah and Dewa Seldzey,
The hundred thousandfold assembly of anuyoga
    masters,
I supplicate you; bestow your blessings and siddhis.

Lilavajra and Buddhaguhya,
Leykyi Wangmo and eight vidyadharas,
Great charioteers of the tantra and sadhana sections,
I supplicate you; bestow your blessings and siddhis.

Vidyamantra adepts of kriya, charya, and yoga,
Ornaments and supreme ones of Jambudvipa along
    with your wondrous disciples,
Eminent lamps who illuminate the Muni's teachings,
I supplicate you; bestow your blessings and siddhis.

Pervading lord of the ocean of the three roots,
    Thotreng Tsal,
Eight supreme aspects and twelve manifestations,
Inconceivable circle of the magical net,
I supplicate you; bestow your blessings and siddhis.

Vimalamitra and Khenchen Bodhisattva,
Dharma king, father and sons, Vairotsana and Tsogyal,
Incarnated king and disciples, assembly of translators
    and panditas,
I supplicate you; bestow your blessings and siddhis.

So, Zur, Nub, and Nyang along with the ocean of
    tertons,
Dharma emperors of kama, terma, and pure visions,
Learned and accomplished ones, appearing successively
    throughout the three times,
I supplicate you; bestow your blessings and siddhis.

Superior and noble wisdom body, embodiment of all
    refuges,
Perceived by disciples as a supreme teacher,
Root guru of incomparable kindness,
I supplicate you; bestow your blessings and siddhis.

Vajrasattva, deities of Dupa and Gyutrul,
Nine glorious herukas, five and three families,
Yidam deities of the six sections of tantra,
I supplicate you; bestow your blessings and siddhis.

Shakyamuni, supreme guide of beings in the Good
    Kalpa,
Perfect buddhas, guides of the ten directions and four
    times,

Countless ones appearing as the nirmanakaya to tame
  whoever needs to be tamed,
I supplicate you; bestow your blessings and siddhis.

Comprised of the truths of cessation and of the path,
Calm desireless and uncompounded nectar,
Ocean of the collections of the nine gradual vehicles,
I supplicate you; bestow your blessings and siddhis.

Ajita, Manjushri, Vajrapani, and Lokeshvara,
Samantabhadra and so forth, Mahayana beings,
All the noble Sangha of shravakas and
  pratyekabuddhas,
I supplicate you; bestow your blessings and siddhis.

Dakas and dakinis of the three abodes,
Vajra Dharma protectors, wealth gods, and treasure lords,
Infinite oceanlike assemblage of objects of refuge,
I supplicate you; bestow your blessings and siddhis.

I supplicate you, precious jewels,
Grant your blessings, assemblage of vidyadhara gurus.
Bestow your siddhis, peaceful and wrathful yidam
  deities,
Dispel all obstacles, dakinis and Dharma protectors.

Thinking of you with intense longing from my heart,
I bow down and make offerings with one-pointed
  devotion.

With faith I take refuge and pledge to be your servant.
Accept me and sustain me with your compassion.

Having fully purified my being of the two veils and
their tendencies,
Increase my life span, merit, splendor, wealth,
experience, realization, and wisdom.
Ripening and freeing the minds of countless other
disciples,
Bestow your blessings so that we may perfect the activity
of all the buddhas.

May all the sacred lamps of the Buddha's teachings,
without bias,
Live for hundreds of aeons turning the wheel of the
Dharma.
Bestow your blessings so that the Sangha and the
splendor of the teachings of exposition and practice
May flourish and spread in all directions.

May the degeneration of the dark age cease for all
worlds and beings,
And may happiness and Dharmic wealth spontaneously
increase.
Bestow your blessings so that everyone may enter the
gate of the Supreme Essence Vehicle
And accomplish the state of the four kayas.

Although I've not yet achieved that state in my many
lives,
May I never be separated from the mind of
enlightenment.
Bestow your blessings that I may master the ocean of
bodhisattva deeds
And establish myself and others in well-being and
happiness.

In short, from now until supreme enlightenment,
Objects of refuge, lords of wisdom and compassion,
Constantly accept me, grant your blessings,
And create the auspicious circumstance in which
the virtuous goodness of existence and peace will
increase.
SARVA SUSHRIYA SIDDHI BHAVATU.

*Emphasizing the tradition of the Vajra Vehicle of the Early Translations,
this supplication was offered by Khyentse Wangpo, a joyful servant of Guru
Padma.*

THE MIGHTY VAJRADHARA
OF THE DEFINITIVE MEANING

A Spontaneous Song

Dudjom Rinpoche

The mighty Vajradhara of the definitive meaning,
The ultimate realization of Samantabhadra,
Is directly pointed out as my natural face by the guru.
I remember my guide who is like a second Garab Dorje.
The excellent path of dzogchen
Is the heart of the eighty-four thousand teachings of the
    victorious ones.
To naturally liberate without abandoning the deluded
    thoughts of fixation—
This is the greatness of the oral instructions.
There is no choosing between the phenomena of
    samsara and nirvana.

Young Dudjom Rinpoche

When reassuming the natural abode in our innate essence,
The king of fruition is discovered to be within.
What a joy to accomplish the aims of a happy mind!
While realizing that self-awareness is the guru,
I supplicate him with free-flowing naturalness.
Cutting through the straying of conceptual mind,
Let us arrive at the state of nonmeditation.
By the power and blessings of the ocean of victorious
ones and their children,
And by the aspirations of all sages accomplished in
true speech,
May the life of Master Tubten Kunga Gyaltsen be
long
And his activity spread to the ends of the world.

This was written by Jigdrel Yeshe.

Mahamudra

Illuminating Wisdom

Milarepa

Homage to all the sacred masters.

When we talk about the characteristics of the mahamudra of illuminating wisdom, we talk about three sections: ground mahamudra, path mahamudra, and fruition mahamudra.

First, the ground mahamudra—the essential nature of things, the mind of the buddhas, the mind-essence of sentient beings—does not exist as something that has color or shape, a center or edge. It is free from limitations and partiality, and knows neither existence nor nonexistence. It is neither confused nor liberated. It is not created by causes and not changed by conditions. It is neither altered by the wisdom of the buddhas nor spoiled by the obscurations of sentient beings. It is neither improved by realization nor worsened by confusion.

Path mahamudra is that which is to be practiced within the ground mahamudra as follows: When settling, settle without conceptualizing. When remaining, remain without distraction. When practicing, practice without fixation.

When manifesting, let it manifest as dharmata. When freed, practice it as natural freedom.

Beyond concepts, fruition mahamudra is free from something that liberates, free from hope and fear. It is the exhaustion of concepts and phenomena; it is nonfixation, nongrasping, and it is free from utterance and description and is thus beyond concept.

Ground, path, and fruition are to be practiced as one.

This instruction on the illuminating wisdom of mahamudra was composed by the yogi Milarepa.

Gampopa

THE SINGLE SUFFICIENT PATH

Gampopa

Homage to all the sacred masters.

This instruction, entitled "Gampopa's Single Sufficient Path of Mahamudra," has three parts:

1. Resolving the natural state.
2. Pointing out the mode-of-being.
3. Training in thatness as the path.

The first section, resolving the natural state, has five points:

- Mahamudra has no cause.
- Mahamudra has no condition.
- Mahamudra has no method.
- Mahamudra has no path.
- Mahamudra has no fruition.

The second section, pointing out the mode-of-being, has five points:

- Mahamudra has no cause, yet faith and devotion are the cause.

- Mahamudra has no condition, yet a sacred master is the condition.
- Mahamudra has no method, yet nonfabrication is the method.
- Mahamudra has no path, yet undistracted mind is the path.
- Mahamudra has no fruition, yet freeing concepts into dharmata is the fruition.

The third section, training in thatness as the path, has four points:

1. As a preliminary, practice the guru yoga three times during the day and three times at night with faith, devotion, and respectfulness.
2. As the main practice, settle the mind in the state of nonfabrication and embrace it with nondistraction.
3. As a conclusion, recognize whatever occurs as being your own mind and train your awareness in that recognition.
4. Training in the way in which experiences manifest, exert yourself in meditation practice until concepts have been exhausted.

There are two types of experiences that occur: disturbing and harmonious. The former include dullness, excitement, sickness, fear, jadedness, doubt, and so forth. Since they result from practice, no matter which of these may occur, recognize them to be temporary experiences. Without trying to discard these experiences, make them the aim of your view and meditation. Henceforth, harmonious experiences will naturally occur. The first harmonious experience is the occurrence of stillness; from this, the experience of the empty essence follows. Next comes the experience of attainment, and finally the experience of revulsion. Exert yourself in meditation practice. Do not regard the way in which experience and realization occur to be enough. Beyond this, it is not enough for your mind to be still; you must practice seeing its essence. It is not enough to only see its essence; you must practice to attain realization. It is not enough to attain realization; you must practice to turn from attachment. It is not enough to only turn away from attachment; you must practice to free your conceptual mind in dharmata and attain buddhahood in the exhaustion of phenomena and concepts.

Thus spoke Gampopa. This completes the heart essence, "The Single Sufficient Path of Mahamudra," which was first transmitted by the great pandita Lord Naropa.

Karmapa Rangjung Dorje

THE MAHAMUDRA ASPIRATION
OF TRUE MEANING

Karmapa Rangjung Dorje

NAMO GURU
All masters and yidam deities of the mandalas,
Victorious ones and spiritual children throughout the
three times and ten directions,
Pay heed to me and bestow your blessings
That I may fulfill my aspirations.

Springing forth from the snow mountain of the pure
thoughts and deeds
Of myself and all countless beings,
May streams of virtue, undefiled by the three concepts,
Flow into the ocean of the four kayas of the victorious
ones.

For as long as this has not been attained,
May we, throughout our successive lives and rebirths,

Never even hear the words "misdeeds" or "suffering"
But enjoy this splendorous ocean of happiness and
   virtue.

Having obtained the supreme freedoms and riches,
   possessing faith, perseverance, and intelligence,
We have followed an eminent spiritual guide and
   received the nectar of oral instructions.
Free of all obstacles to accomplishing them correctly,
May we, in all our lives, practice the sacred teachings.

By learning the scriptures and through reasoning, we
   are freed from the veil of ignorance.
By contemplating the oral instructions, we overcome the
   darkness of doubt.
With the light resulting from meditation, we illuminate
   the natural state as it is.
May the light of this threefold knowledge increase.

Through the nature of the ground, the two truths free
   from the extremes of eternalism and nihilism,
And the supreme path, the two accumulations free from
   the limits of exaggeration and denigration,
We attain the fruition of the two benefits free from the
   extremes of existence and quiescence.
May we connect with such a teaching free from error.

The ground of purification is mind-essence, the union of
being empty and cognizant.
That which purifies is the great vajralike practice of
mahamudra.
May we realize the immaculate dharmakaya, the
fruition of having purified
All the passing stains of confusion that are to be
purified.

To have cut one's misconceptions of the ground is the
confidence of the view.
To sustain this without distraction is the key point of
meditation.
To train in all the points of practice is the supreme
action.
May we possess the confidence of view, meditation, and
action.

All phenomena are the illusory display of mind.
Mind is devoid of "mind"—empty of any entity.
Empty and yet unceasing, it manifests as anything
whatsoever.
Realizing this completely, may we cut its basis and its
root.

We have mistaken our nonexistent personal experience
to be objects,
And by the power of ignorance, mistaken self-
cognizance to be a "self."

This dualistic fixation has made us wander in the sphere
of samsaric existence.
May we cut ignorance and confusion at its very root.

It is not existent since even the victorious ones do not see
it.
It is not nonexistent since it is the basis of samsara and
nirvana.
This is not a contradiction, but the middle way of unity.
May we realize the nature of mind, free from extremes.

No one can indicate it by saying, "This is it."
No one can deny it by saying, "This is not it."
This nature, transcending concepts, is uncompounded.
May we realize this view of true meaning.

Without realizing this, we circle through the ocean of
samsara.
When realizing it, buddhahood is not somewhere else.
It is completely devoid of "it is this" or "it is not this."
May we see this vital point of the all-ground, the nature
of things.

Perceiving is mind; being empty is also mind.
Realizing is mind; being mistaken is also mind.
Having arisen is mind; having ceased is also mind.
May we cut through all our doubts concerning mind.

Unspoiled by intellectual and deliberate meditation,
And unmoved by the winds of ordinary distractions,
May we be skilled in sustaining the practice of mind-
  essence
And be able to rest in unfabricated and innate
  naturalness.

The waves of gross and subtle thoughts having
  spontaneously subsided,
The river of unwavering mind naturally abides.
Free from the stains of dullness, sluggishness, and
  conceptualization,
May we be stable in the unmoving ocean of shamatha.

When looking again and again into the unseen mind,
The fact that there is nothing to see is vividly seen as it is.
Cutting through doubts about its nature being existent
  or nonexistent,
May we unmistakenly recognize our own essence.

When observing objects, they are seen to be the mind,
  devoid of objects.
When observing the mind, there is no mind, as it is
  empty of any entity.
When observing both, dualistic fixation is spontaneously
  freed.
May we realize the luminous nature of mind.

Being free from mental fabrication, it is mahamudra.
Devoid of extremes, it is the great middle way.
It is also called dzogchen, the embodiment of all.
May we attain the confidence of realizing all by
    knowing one nature.

Great bliss, free from attachment, is unceasing.
Luminosity, devoid of fixation, is unobscured.
Nonthought, transcending the intellect, is spontaneously
    present.
Without effort, may our experience be unceasing.

The fixation of clinging to good experiences is
    spontaneously freed.
The confusion of bad thoughts is naturally purified.
Ordinary mind is free from acceptance and rejection.
May we realize the truth of dharmata, devoid of
    constructs.

The nature of all beings is always the enlightened state.
But, because of not realizing it, they wander endlessly in
    samsara.
Towards the countless sentient beings who suffer,
May overwhelming compassion arise in our minds.

The play of overwhelming compassion being
    unobstructed,
In the moment of love, the empty essence nakedly
    dawns.

May we constantly practice day and night
This supreme path of unity, devoid of errors.

The eyes and superknowledges resulting from the
    power of practice,
The ripening of sentient beings, the cultivation of
    buddha realms,
And the perfection of aspirations to accomplish all
    enlightened qualities—
May we attain the buddhahood of having accomplished
    perfection, ripening, and cultivation.

By the power of the compassion of the victorious ones
And their children in the ten directions,
And by all the perfect virtue that exists,
May I and all beings attain accomplishment in
    accordance with these aspirations.

THE VIEW, MEDITATION, AND ACTION OF MAHAMUDRA

Tsokdrug Rangdrol

NAMO GURU PRABHAKARAYE.

Lord Drukpa, embodiment of all the unfailing objects
    of refuge,
Now and always, I supplicate you.
If you want to create good Dharma habits,
I shall now speak a few sincere words as a Dharma link.
In general, only now have we acquired a human body.
In particular, it is extremely rare to receive the threefold
    precepts.
If we don't endeavor in Dharma practice correctly
Now that we have acquired a human body,
It will be hard to find such a body in the future.
Therefore practice prostrations and circumambulations
    while you still can.
Our enemy, Yama the Lord of Death, is all-powerful.

It is never certain when he will come for you.
You may intend to do some Dharma practice, but death
overtakes you.
Therefore, without delay, abandon misdeeds and do
what is virtuous.
Simply hearing of the sufferings of the three lower
realms
Sets our hearts aquiver.
When they actually befall us, what will we do?
Considering that, avoid misdeeds as if they were poison.
While caught in these endless sufferings of samsara,
The ones who can truly give refuge are the Three
Jewels.
Constantly supplicate them from your hearts.
All sentient beings among the six classes
Have been our parents in many past lives.
How they suffer here in these samsaric realms!
Dedicate to their welfare whatever Dharma practice
you do.
Visualize the perfect lord guru above your head.
Regard him as truly being the essence that is the single
embodiment
Of all the buddhas of the realms in the ten directions
and the three times.
Supplicate him from deep within your heart.
Let him melt into light, and mingle your minds
together.
Without altering it, rest precisely in that state.

The mind does not exist; it is not a concrete thing.
It is not nonexistent; anything can be thought.
Sometimes the mind is quiet; sometimes it thinks.
You should always keep a watch on your mind.
Your mind, its essence empty,
Is the mental dharmakaya, Amitabha.
Your mind, its nature luminous,
Is the mental sambhogakaya, the Great Compassionate
    One.
Your mind, the thinker of all things,
Is the mental nirmanakaya, Padmakara.
If you recognize it, it is the five buddhas.
When your mind is cognizant, look into the essence of
    cognizance—
That is mahamudra of cognizant emptiness.
When your mind is blissful, look into the essence of this
    bliss—
That is dzogchen of blissful emptiness.
When your mind is empty, look into the natural face of
    this emptiness—
That is the great madhyamaka of aware emptiness.
When your mind is afraid, look into the essence of that
    which is afraid—
That is the sacred teaching of the chö practice.
Your mind that is empty of all concreteness,
That is the empty mind, transcendent knowledge.
Look into your mind whether you walk or whether
    you sit;

Then walking and sitting are the real
circumambulations.
Look into your mind whether you eat or whether you
drink;
Then eating and drinking are the undefiled feast
offering.
Look into your mind whether you lie down or whether
you sleep;
That is the instruction in recognizing the luminosity of
sleep.
When you are practicing the sadhanas of profound
teachings,
Look into your own mind, the profound meaning;
That will avert the maras and obstacles.
Whatever fleeting acts you do right now,
Do them as you would practice in the final moment of
death.
Whatever activities occur that beguile your mind,
Such as the talk and spectacles of many people,
Don't fall under the power of distraction;
But without forgetting, be persistently mindful
And practice this, the key point of profound meditation.
Develop stability in that very mindfulness.
To be able to realize this again and again,
Is to be accustomed to the practice of meditation.
Over time, by practicing these points,
Your meditation will become continuous, beyond
sessions and breaks,

Uninterrupted, like the flow of a river.
These words are but an auspicious coincidence for that
    to occur.

*Tsokdrug Rangdrol composed this oral instruction in the style of the
view, meditation, and action of mahamudra in response to the request of
Ngawang Kunga Tendzin, the most recent incarnation of Karma Tenphel.*

NOTES ON MAHAMUDRA

Pema Karpo

Homage to the precious Kagyü masters.

Here—under the three headings of preliminaries, main part, and conclusion—I shall explain the instructions in unifying coemergent mahamudra, which points out the stream of ordinary mind to be perfect wakefulness.

PRELIMINARIES

There are two types of preliminaries—general and specific—of which the general preliminaries are explained elsewhere. First, practice the steps of refuge and *bodhichitta* up to guru yoga.

Then for the specific preliminaries, follow the *Abhisambodhi of Vairochana.*[3]

> *Straighten your body and assume the vajra posture.*
> *One-pointed mind is mahamudra.*

---

3. The sevenfold posture of Vairochana.

Thus, place your legs in the vajra posture and your hands below the navel in the gesture of equanimity. Straighten the spinal column. Turn out the inside of the arms. Crook your neck like a hook, the chin lightly pressing the larynx. Touch the tongue to the palate. In general, the attention is led by the sense organs, but in particular by the eyes, so without blinking or moving them, look straight ahead, the distance of an oxen yoke. These points are known as the sevenfold posture of Vairochana, and, in regard to their function, they are called the five attributes of concentration.

Specifically, the cross-legged posture ensures that the downward-clearing wind enters the central channel. The gesture of equanimity ensures this for the fire-equalizing wind; straightening the backbone and turning the inside of the arms out does so for the pervading wind; crooking the neck does so for the upward-moving wind; and touching the tongue to the palate and maintaining the gaze does so for the life-sustaining wind. When these five winds enter the central channel, all other winds will have entered the central channel too, and nonconceptual wakefulness will dawn. This is called "remaining in the solitude of body," "remaining with unmoving body," or "remaining in the naturalness of body."

For speech, not to talk after having expelled the stale breath is called "remaining in the solitude of speech," "remaining with unmoving speech," or "remaining in the naturalness of speech."

Don't reflect on the past. Don't imagine the future. Don't meditate with deliberate conceptual labeling. And don't regard emptiness as being nothingness. Without evaluating as right or wrong any of the objects of the five senses you perceive, face inward and, leaving your attention in naturalness, remain naturally just like an infant. Don't let your attention wander for even an instant.

> *Completely abandoning the thinker and what is thought,*
> *Remain naturally like a child.*
> *If you diligently apply yourself to the words of the guru,*
> *The coemergent will surely dawn.*

Tilopa also said:

> *Don't reflect, don't imagine, and don't evaluate. Don't*
> *meditate, don't think, rest in naturalness.*

The king of the Dharma, *Dawoe Shonnu*[4] said, "Nondistraction is the path of all buddhas." This is called "resting in the solitude of mind," "resting with unmoving mind," or "resting in the naturalness of mind."

Nagarjuna said:

> *Wangchuk, it is taught that mindfulness of the body*
> *Is the single path traversed by the sugatas.*
> *Concentrate and be truly observant,*
> *Because losing mindfulness destroys all Dharma practice.*

As the Abhidharma mentions, this mindfulness means nondistraction: "Mindfulness is not to forget the related object."

---

4. Another of Gampopa's names.

THE MAIN PART

The second topic, the main part, has two sections: general practices and specific practices.

The General Practices

There are two divisions to the general practices: the root of meditation, training in the yoga of one-pointedness after experiencing shamatha; and training in the yoga of simplicity by identifying *vipashyana* after examining the root of stillness and thinking.

THE ROOT OF MEDITATION:
TRAINING IN THE YOGA OF ONE-POINTEDNESS
AFTER EXPERIENCING SHAMATHA

This has two parts: supported and unsupported. Supported shamatha is either without or with the use of *prana*. For the support without prana, there is the impure type by taking the support of a pebble or stick and the pure type by taking the support of the body, speech, or mind of the *tathagatas*.

- I -[5]

First, when using the impure support of a pebble or stick, place a small stone in front of you to focus upon and look one-pointedly at nothing but it without letting your attention project outwardly or concentrate inwardly. Imagine your guru at the crown of your head and think he is a buddha in

---

5. These numbers appear in the Tibetan manuscript and denote the progressive order of the meditations.

PERFECT CLARITY

person. Make the "Manam Khama"[6] the supreme attainment of mahamudra! Receive these siddhis and dissolve your guru into you. Imagine that his mind is mingled with yours, and rest for as long as you remain in equanimity.

Keep training while telling your guru about the character of your mental states as they occur. If dull, raise your gaze and train in a more open environment. When lethargic, concentrate by remembering the previous points. If agitated, stay in a secluded place, lower the gaze, and place emphasis on looseness.

- 2 -

Next, "using the pure support of the body, speech, and mind of the tathagatas" means to take the support of an image as the body, a syllable as the speech, or a sphere as the mind.

First, for using the support of an image as the body in front of you, keep your attention constantly focused upon a molded image, a painting, or a golden Buddha statue that resembles pure gold, is adorned with the major and minor marks, is radiant, and wears the three Dharma robes.

- 3 -

Secondly, for using the support of a syllable as the speech, imagine, in front of you, a moon disc the size of a fingernail upon which is the letter HUNG, as if drawn with a single hair.

---

6. This is most probably the supplication that reminds us that we are doing practice for "*all sentient beings, my mothers, whose number is unfathomable like the sky.*"

- 4 -

Third, for using the support of a sphere as the mind, just as before, keep your attention fixed upon an egg-shaped sphere, the size of a pea, which is endowed with the special attribute of shining with rays of light.

- 5 -

Next, for shamatha employing prana, there is using the support of vajra recitation and using the support of the vase breath.

First, when using the support of vajra recitation, let your body and mind rest in naturalness. Then focus your attention on the inhalation and exhalation of the breath and, without applying anything else, count them as one, two, and so forth, up to 21,600. By doing so you will become familiar with the number of in and out movements of the breath.

- 6 -

Following that, for as long as the inhalation and exhalation last, follow the inhalation and exhalation of your breath with the notion, "Does it move from the body as a whole or from a single area?" By doing so you will become familiar with the characteristics of the breath.

- 7 -

Next, mingle your breathing and attention together and observe the character of going, coming, and remaining from the tip of your nose to the navel. By doing this you will perceive the exact color and duration of the individual breaths.

Then examine the five major elements, individually and distinctly. By doing so you will understand the increase and decrease in the inward and outward movement of the breath.

Next, transform the outward movement of the breath into the white syllable OM, the inward movement into the blue letter HUNG, and the remaining into the red syllable AH. By doing so you will realize the ceasing of the inward and outward movement of the breath.

Second, to use the support of the vase breath, expel the stale breath three times, and gently inhale the upper prana through the nose. Draw up the lower prana and exert yourself in retaining it as long as you are able. In this way, since the so-called mind that is extremely difficult to tame is not found apart from the prana, when the movement of prana ceases, the conceptual thinking that is your attention fluttering after objects will also come to a halt.

Next, there are three types of unsupported shamatha, namely the key points of directly cutting the sudden arising, leaving whatever takes place without fabrication, and the method of letting be.

11

First is directly cutting the sudden arising. After having trained in the above methods, when a thought arises, meaning that your attention moves toward an object, don't allow it to continue but focus attentively while thinking, "I must not give rise to a single thought!" Thus train in directly cutting the pursuit of suddenly arising thoughts.

- 12 -

By training in this way, you will seem to have more and more thoughts, and, finally, they will appear to be unceasing as they arise one after the other. This is called "acknowledging thoughts like recognizing one's enemy" and is also known as the first stage of stillness, like a waterfall on a mountain cliff. In other words, you perceive the arising and ceasing of thoughts because the attention remains still for a mere moment. You only seem to have more thoughts, but in fact they are no more or less, because thoughts arise incessantly since it is the nature of things that a thought arises in one instant and ceases in the next.

- 13 -

Second, for leaving whatever takes place without fabrication, allow the thought to do as it pleases. Don't be governed by it, and don't try to thwart it. Train in placing your attention on guard. By training in this way, you will cease to pursue the thought and will remain one-pointedly in stillness.

- 14 -

Following that, another thought will suddenly stir and you should repeat the above process. When the continuity of the stillness lasts longer and longer, it is known as the second stage of stillness, like the gentle flow of a river.

Through this key point of resting freely, you separate

the pure attention from the impure, as the Lord of Dharma [Gampopa] said:

When unmodified, attention settles.
When undisturbed, water clears.

The great Lord of Yogis [Lingrepa] said:

When letting be in unmodified freshness, realization dawns.
When sustaining it like the flow of a river, it achieves
  fullness.
Completely abandon all reference points and attributes!
Yogis, remain in constant equanimity!

About these two methods Saraha said:

When bound, the mind tries to roam in the ten directions.
When set free, it remains in unmoving steadiness.
I have realized this camel-like paradox.

Third, for the key point of the method of letting be, there are four parts.

- 15 -

First, letting be like a brahman braiding a thread. Just as such a brahman must keep a balance between tight and loose, when the meditation training is too concentrated you stray into thinking and when too slack you remain sluggish. Therefore maintain a balance between tight and loose. In other words, a beginner should at first concentrate by directly cutting the sudden arising, and then when tired of that, loosen by leaving whatever takes place without fabrication. Alternating in this way, after a while there will be a natural balance between tight and loose. That is why it is taught to focus the attention tightly and then release it loosely like, a brahman braiding a thread.

- 16 -

Second is letting be like cutting the cord on a bundle of straw. All these previous remedies essentially come down to thinking, "A thought has arisen, so I must remain undistracted!" The remedy is therefore not successful unless the thought has stopped. This is called a trailing mindfulness and is an impure form of meditation. So, to leave behind such mindfulness and naturally and simply let be in the continuity of stillness is called "leaving the attention effortlessly, like cutting the cord on a bundle of straw."

- 17 -

Third is letting be like a child looking in a shrine hall. Tying the elephant of mind tightly to the pole of mindfulness, the pranas are captured in themselves. Due to this, no matter what temporary manifestation you may experience—empty forms such as smoke and so forth, almost fainting with bliss, or a state of nonthought, as if sitting in midair feeling that you have no body or mind—not reacting in any way, such as becoming elated and deliberately fixating on it, or else treating it as a defect and trying to inhibit the experience, is called "leaving the experience unobstructed without fixation like a child looking in a shrine hall."

- 18 -

Fourth, letting be like an elephant being pricked by a thorn means that a thought arising within stillness coincides with the mindfulness that recognizes it. When the object to be abandoned is blended together with its remedy, one thought is unable to lead to another. The remedy occurring by itself, without the need for cultivating it with effort, is known as a retained mindfulness and that is the meaning of letting be without trying to prevent or cultivate thoughts and sense impressions, like an elephant being pricked by a thorn. This is also taught to be the third stage of stillness, like the ocean free from waves.

Recognizing thinking within stillness and seizing the natural seat of stillness within the occurrence of thoughts is therefore called "intermingling stillness and occurrence," and hence is also called the "recognition of one-pointedness."

At this point, that which recognizes the stillness and thought occurrence is called correct reflection, discriminating knowledge, or self-awareness. About this the *Ornament of the Sutras* says:

Hence you will attain
The great pliancy of body and mind
Known as reflection and discernment.

TRAINING IN THE YOGA OF SIMPLICITY BY IDENTIFYING VIPASHYANA AFTER EXAMINING THE ROOT OF STILLNESS AND THINKING

This has three parts: examining the root of stillness, identifying vipashyana, and training in the yoga of simplicity.

Examining the Root of Stillness and Thinking

- 19 -

During stillness, you should now examine the nonconceptual shamatha that arises as discriminating knowledge. What is the identity of this stillness? How does it remain still? What is the movement of the thought arising within? During a thought occurrence, does a thought occur after the stillness has faded, or while stillness remains? Is the occurrence something apart from the stillness or not? What is its identity? How does it finally cease?

- 20 -

Since you cannot define the occurrence as anything other than the stillness moving, and the stillness as anything other than the occurrence remaining still, you fail to find an entity that is still or that moves.

So next, examine the noticing that watches with the eyes of natural awareness. Is it different from the stillness or occurrence that is observed, or is it the stillness and occurrence itself? By doing so you fail to find anything at all, and the observer and the observed are discovered to be indivisible. And since the identity cannot be defined as anything whatsoever, it is called "the view that transcends concepts" or "the view beyond assertion." The King of the Victorious Ones therefore declared:

> *A conceptually made view, even if eminent, still perishes.*
> *Transcending concepts, even the word* view *vanishes.*
> *The observer and the observed are indivisible.*
> *This certainty I have found through the kindness of the*
>   *guru.*

The master Shantideva spoke of this very type of analysis when he said,

When exerting yourself in samadhi
Without straying for even an instant,
Examine your mind in this way,
"What is this mind that analyzes?"

Using the analogy of firewood and flames, it is said in the
Sutra Requested by Kashyapa:

Rubbing two sticks together, flames appear
Burning away both sticks.
Similarly, when the faculty of discriminating knowledge
arises,
That which arises burns duality away.

Since this type of analysis entails examining by means of
a natural awareness that looks into itself, it is known as the
analytical meditation of a kusulu, a simple meditator. It dif-
fers from the analytical meditations of a pandita, or scholar,
which involves examining by means of an attention that looks
away from itself.

Identifying Vipashyana

- 21 -

Second, for identifying vipashyana, no matter what thought
or disturbing emotion arises, do not try to cast it away and
do not be governed by it; instead, leave whatever is experienced without fabrication. When you recognize it the very
moment it arises, it itself dawns as emptiness that is basic
purity without abandonment. In this way you are able to uti-

lize all adversity as the path, and this is therefore called "taking adversity as the path."

Your realization that objects to be abandoned and their remedies are indivisible, since thoughts are liberated by simply recognizing them, is the heart of Vajrayana practice and is called "training in exorcism."

At this point, you should feel an even greater compassion for all those sentient beings who do not realize the nature of their own minds. While you spend your life practicing the methods (*upaya*) such as the development stage with your body, speech, and mind for the sake of all sentient beings, it is through this type of discriminating knowledge (*prajna*) that, having utterly purified any clinging to the reality of negative emotions, you will avoid falling prey to them. It is just like remaining unharmed when eating a poison that has been blessed by a mantra.

It is with this type of practice in mind that the following words were spoken: "Neither accept nor reject whatever arises on the path!"

Training in the Yoga of Simplicity

- 22 -

This has three parts: examining in terms of the three times, examining in terms of being concrete or inconcrete, and examining in terms of being singular or multiple.

First is examining in terms of the three times: Past thoughts have ceased and disappeared, future thoughts have neither arisen nor appeared, and present thoughts cannot be pinpointed in any way whatsoever. Analyzing in this way, scrutinize the nature of all phenomena. Understand this notion: "Everything is devoid of reality and is merely labeled by one's own mind and therefore possesses no arising, ceasing, or remaining!" As Saraha said,

> *When that which arises as concrete has completely subsided,*
> *like the sky,*
> *All concreteness is abandoned—so what can arise after that?*
> *Today, through the guru's teachings, I realized*
> *That everything has the primordial nature of nonarising.*

You should analyze in that way.

- 23 -

Second, examining in terms of being concrete or inconcrete means to analyze as follows: "Does my mind exist as something concrete or is it nonexistent and inconcrete? If it has concreteness, what are the perceiver and perceived made of? If it is perceptible, then what is its shape and color? Is the perceiver, too, nothing more than a seeming presence? If it is inconcrete then what creates these countless kinds of perceptions?" In such an analysis, you could quite rightly define mind as a concrete thing if it were comprised of some entity, but since, in the face of intelligent analysis, it is not comprised of anything whatsoever, you don't find any existent, concrete thing that defines it. However, since it is experienced by self-cognizant wakefulness, it should not be categorized as nonexistent and inconcrete.

Consequently, transcending both concreteness and inconcreteness, it is known as the middle way that doesn't fall into the extremes of eternalism or nihilism.

As is said,

For those who take the guru's words to heart,
It is like seeing a treasure in the palm of one's hand.

- 24 -

Third, examining in terms of being singular or multiple means to examine as follows: Is the mind one or multiple? If the mind is one, then how can it be discerned as myriad experiences? If it is multiple, then how can all these experiences be equal in that their nature is emptiness? By analyzing in this way, discovering that the mind is beyond both distinctions and the freedom from extremes is called "the mahamudra of complete nondwelling."

In the meditation state of the practitioner who has realized this, there is no appearance other than individual, self-cognizant wakefulness. It is therefore known as the absence of appearance. Since, during the post-meditation state, this path purifies clinging to phenomena as being real, it is called "appearance like a magical illusion."

As is said,

In front, behind, and in the ten directions,
Whatever is seen is just that.
Today the guru has cut through my delusion
So now I have nothing further to ask anyone.

The Specific Practices

There are two types of specific practices: the yoga of one taste, equalizing the taste of all phenomena into the indivisibility of appearance and mind; and the yoga of nonmeditation, establishing all phenomena as being the innate coemergence of dharmakaya.

THE YOGA OF ONE TASTE:
EQUALIZING THE TASTE OF ALL PHENOMENA INTO
THE INDIVISIBILITY OF APPEARANCE AND MIND

This has three parts:

- Pointing out that appearances are mind through the analogy of sleep and dreaming.
- Pointing out that appearance and emptiness are a unity through the analogy of water and ice.
- Establishing that all phenomena are of one taste through the analogy of water and waves.

- 25 -

First, pointing out that appearances are mind through the analogy of sleep and dreaming is as follows. Just as everything experienced during sleep is nothing other than your mind, all your present experiences are just a dream after falling into the sleep of ignorance, and hence they are merely your own mind. Consequently, by resting loosely in simply experiencing whatever object may appear, externally perceived objects and your own mind mingle into one taste without being split into two. The Lord of Yogis described this:

Your experience of last night's dream
Is the teacher who points out that appearances are mind.
Do you understand that this is so?

Moreover:

Change the color of everything in the three realms, without
    exception,
Into the same great state of passion.

- 26 -

Second, pointing out that appearance and emptiness are a unity through the analogy of water and ice is as follows. All these phenomena, no matter how they are experienced, are empty because, from the very moment they arise, they lack an inherent identity of their own. Yet, while not consisting of anything whatsoever, they are experienced in countless ways. This is known as the unity or one taste of appearance and emptiness, like the analogy of ice and water.

Similarly, understanding that bliss and emptiness, luminosity and emptiness, and awareness and emptiness are also unities is called "realizing multiplicity as being one taste." As is said,

When realizing, everything is just that.
No one will discover anything other than that.
This is study; it is also reflection and meditation training.

- 27 -

Third is establishing that all phenomena are of one taste through the analogy of water and waves. Just like a wave is but the rising of the water, understand that all phenomena are created by means of the emptiness of your own mind arising in all forms. Saraha said:

No matter what the mind projects,
It still has the nature of the guru.

The intrinsic nature (*dharmata*) permeating the realm of phenomena (*dharmadhatu*) is known as one taste manifesting as multiplicity. The practitioner who realizes this experiences all-pervading emptiness during the ensuing wakefulness.

THE YOGA OF NONMEDITATION: ESTABLISHING ALL PHENOMENA AS BEING THE INNATE COEMERGENCE OF DHARMAKAYA

- 28 -

To train in this, since any disturbing emotions to be abandoned are already exhausted, the antidotes that overcome them are also exhausted, and thus the path has ceased. As there is nowhere else to go, the journey has ceased. There is no progress beyond this; thus you attain the nondwelling nirvana, the supreme accomplishment of mahamudra. This is described in the *Root Scripture on Mingling*:

Kyeho!
This is self-cognizant wakefulness!
It is beyond words and not an object of the mind.
I, Tilopa, have nothing whatsoever to show you.
Understand that you see this yourself!

Moreover:

Don't reflect, don't imagine, and don't evaluate,
Don't meditate, don't think, rest in naturalness.

That is how it is.

THE CONCLUSION

For this there are three parts:

1. Identifying mahamudra and pointing out the natural face.
2. Examining hindrances and deviations.
3. Distinguishing theoretical understanding, experience, and realization.

- 29 -

First, for identifying mahamudra and pointing out the natural face, there are the following points:

- Ascertaining the ground.
- Training in the path.
- Distinguishing the subtle experiences.
- Identifying the signs of progress of the paths and *bhumis*.
- The fourfold yoga of the realized fruition.

- 30 -

Second, examining hindrances and deviations is as follows:

- Recognizing that appearances are mind dispels the hindrance of appearances arising as enemies.
- Recognizing that thoughts are dharmakaya dispels the hindrance of conceptual thinking rising up as an enemy.
- Recognizing that appearance and emptiness are a unity dispels the hindrance of emptiness rising up as an enemy.

The three deviations are all due to clinging to the experiences of shamatha, which is expelled by progressing to vipashyana. The four ways of going astray are as follows:

- Letting emptiness arise as compassion cuts through the basic straying from the essence of emptiness.
- Realizing the natural state as it is cuts through the straying into generalization.
- Realizing that the remedy and what is to be relinquished are indivisible prevents the straying into a remedy.
- Realizing that arising and liberation are simultaneous eliminates the straying into a path.

- 31 -

Third is distinguishing theoretical understanding, experience, and realization:

- Realizing the natural state of mind by means of learning and reflection is called theoretical understanding.
- Realizing it one-pointedly in the form of a mental image is called experience.
- Realizing it in actuality, from the stage of simplicity onwards, is known as realization.

Since, in all three cases, the word "realize" means the same thing, there is no conflict in using it throughout.

Accompanied by the gift of more than a bushel of saffron, Shenpen Zangpo, the king of Lahaul and Zangskar requested this from me, stating the need for writing down the notes for mahamudra and the six doctrines. As I thought many fragmentary notes would be unreliable and but a disgrace to the oral tradition, I, Pema Karpo, while staying at Jangchub Nyingpo in the southern district of Kharchu, wrote this solely for the sake of benefitting future generations. May it bring virtuous goodness!

THE INSTRUCTION ON STILLNESS, OCCURRENCE, AND AWARENESS IN MAHAMUDRA

Mipham Rinpoche

If you can simply practice mahamudra and experience stillness, occurrence, and awareness according to the vital instruction of that practice, you will ultimately perceive the truth of reality. This is because the nature of your mind has the sugata essence. Apply the related key instruction.

The basis of all things is mind. After understanding the mind's secret, seek the vital point of your mind and you will become skilled in all things and realize the meaning of egolessness.

Since I am teaching according to the oral instructions of the realized ones, I will leave out various logical investigations. Stillness is when you look into your mind, direct yourself inward, and remain devoid of any kind of thinking. Occurrence is when various kinds of thoughts arise. Awareness is your mind being conscious of either of these.

If you maintain this continuously, you will come to understand the following vital point: Various feelings such as joy and sadness arise from your own mind and dissolve back into your mind. Understanding this, you will come to recognize that all experiences are the personal experiences of your mind.

Subsequently, by looking directly into the essence of your mind, whether it is still or thinking, you will understand that it is empty and, even though it perceives many things, it does not possess any entity whatsoever. This so-called emptiness is not a blank void like space. Rather, you will come to understand that it is an emptiness endowed with all supreme aspects. This means that it does not possess any self-nature, yet it has an unceasing clarity that is fully conscious and cognizant.

When realizing this secret point of mind, although there is no separate watcher or something watched, to experience the naturally luminous and innate mind-essence is known as recognizing awareness. This is what is pointed out in both mahamudra and dzogchen.

According to Saraha, if you can sustain it, "By looking again and again into the primordially pure nature of space, seeing will cease." As stated in the *Prajnaparamita,* "Mind is devoid of mind;[7] the nature of mind is luminous."

There is nothing easier than this, but it is essential to practice.

Composed by Mipham. MANGALAM.

---

7. "Mind is devoid of mind" means that the nature of mind is devoid of dualistic thinking.

DZOGCHEN

Chokgyur Lingpa

THE INSTRUCTION MANUAL FOR THE GROUND OF TREKCHO

Vajra Yogini
Revealed by Chokgyur Lingpa

NAMO GURU DEVA DAKINI[8]

The master endowed with samaya
Should give a worthy disciple
This meditation instruction on the ground of cutting
through, the natural state,
According to the secret practice of dzogchen.

The disciples should arrange feast tormas for the
dakinis,
Offer a red torma to the treasure lords,
And gradually perform the preliminaries for the
instruction.

---

8. The full title of this text reads: *The Instruction Manual for the Ground of Trekcho: What to Carry, Utilize, and Bring Forth on the Path according to "The Secret Dakini Practice: The Mother Tantra of Dzogchen."*

The master should then give the following teaching:

Place your body in the sevenfold posture of Vairochana.
Let the nonarising nature of your mind—this empty
    and luminous awareness, this primordially pure and
    spontaneously present essence—remain in the state of
    the fourfold resting of body, speech, and mind.
Don't pursue what has passed before,
Don't invite what hasn't occurred,
And don't construct present cognizance.

The fourfold resting is:
Rest your body like a corpse in a charnel ground,
    without preference or fixed arrangement.
Rest your voice like a broken waterwheel, in a state of
    stillness.
Rest your eyes like a statue in a shrine room, without
    blinking, in a continuous, focused gaze.
Rest your mind like a sea free from waves, quietly in the
    unfabricated and spontaneously present state of the
    empty and luminous nature of awareness.
Let your mind rest, totally free from thought.

The earth outside, the stones, mountains, rocks, plants,
    trees, and forests do not truly exist.
The body inside does not truly exist.
This empty and luminous mind-nature also does not
    truly exist.

Although it does not truly exist, it cognizes everything.
Thus, to rest in the state of empty and luminous
    awareness is known as the ground of cutting through.

Now, do thoughts occur during this state of stillness?
Is there stillness while the thoughts occur?
There are thoughts during the state of stillness,
And there are four ways of cutting through them:

Like a cat waiting for a mouse,
Look directly into the essence of the thoughts.

Like a brahman threading a needle,
Keep awareness balanced and look into the essence of
    the thoughts.

Like a watchman in a watchtower,
Look into the thoughts within the state of undistracted
    awareness.

Like an arrow flying from an archer,
Look into the thoughts within the state of one-pointed
    awareness.

Now, as for mingling stillness and thinking:
Stillness is to rest quietly in the state of empty and
    luminous mind-nature.
From within that state a thought suddenly occurs.

By looking directly into it, it completely disappears in
the continuity of this mind-nature.
This is called mingling stillness and thinking in the
continuity of mind-nature.

May this meet with a worthy and destined person.

TREASURE SEAL. HIDDEN SEAL. CONCEALED SEAL.
PROFOUND SEAL. SAMAYA. SEAL SEAL SEAL. KHATHAM.

*This is a second copy of the yellow parchment discovered by the kind Kunga
Bum in the Crystal Cave of Drag.*[9]

---

9. The Crystal Cave is situated one day's travel from Samye in Central Tibet.
This teaching was spoken by Vajra Yogini to Yeshe Tsogyal in a dream.
After it was later revealed by Kunga Bum, she handed it over to Dungtso
Repa, himself a terton and great yogi. This transmission, which seems to
have been lost during the centuries, was revived by Chokgyur Lingpa in a
recollection of his former life as Dungtso Repa. The teachings on *The Secret
Dakini Practice: The Mother Tantra of Dzogchen* comprise more than fifty
concise instructions and are now contained in the collection of termas known
as *Chokling Tersar.*

Dudjom Lingpa

Uncultivated Buddhahood

An excerpt from
*An Instruction in Realizing the
Natural Face of Dzogchen*

Dudjom Lingpa

To the omnipresent Primordial Buddha, who is like a sublime city for the magical displays of illusory wisdom manifestations, I prostrate with unswerving devotion.

These days, when the five degenerations are on the rise,[10]
sentient beings find themselves under the powerful sway of
spirits, agitated emotions, and evil karma. They cling to life
though it is but a fleeting dream. They spend their time making long-range plans and preparations as if they were here
for a permanent stay, yet they abandon the pursuit of true,

---

10. The five degenerations are shorter life span, decline in the quality of
things, an increase in disturbing emotions, low and wrong views, and inferior
health and welfare.

lasting benefit. Therefore, those striving for liberation and omniscience are as rare as stars in the daytime.

Even if a few are aware of death and want to practice the Dharma, they spend their lives doing little more than virtuous acts of the physical and verbal variety in pursuit of rebirth as gods or humans. Others, without even the slightest understanding of the view of emptiness, nevertheless conclude that their minds are empty, and so merely identify and acknowledge the nonfabrication of thoughts. By staying inactive in that state, they may be reborn at most as gods in the realms of desire or form, but they will not get even a hairbreadth closer to the path of omniscience.

Therefore, if there is even just a single person who has accumulated a vast stock of merit over countless previous aeons, tethered it to a noble wish, and established a karmic connection to the ultimate teachings, I will explain the following with his good fortune in mind. As for those who lack both a karmic connection to me, as well as the good fortune to master the teachings of dzogchen, they will only slander this doctrine and their minds will flee to the wilderness.

However, you who are not like that, but whose good fortune is equal to my own, ponder these teachings. By examining and becoming familiar with them, recognize samsara and nirvana to be the supreme emptiness, and thus realize your true nature!

Dzogchen contains three sections: mind, space, and instruction. This text belongs to the instruction section and is comprised of view, meditation, and conduct.

First the view is established through these four:

1. Nonexistence (*meypa*)
2. Oneness (*chigpu*)
3. All-pervasiveness (*chalwa*)
4. Spontaneous presence (*lhundrup*)
5. It is crucial to realize that this is, in fact, how it is.

First, to establish the view of nonexistence, there are two parts:

1. Establishing the nonexistence of an individual self.
2. Establishing the nonexistence of a self in things.

That which is called an individual self is simply the feeling of "I exist" during experiences while awake, in dream states, in the *bardo,* and in future lifetimes. The consciousness that had been lying dormant, but which is immediately grasped as "I," is called the secondary consciousness or reflective mind-form. By having such an impression, it comes to appear stable and solid. Hence, by examining the origins of this so-called I, you will discover that it has no source.

Next, in searching for where this so-called I dwells or abides, examine whether any location and separate agent residing there can be identified, and whether it has any characteristics or not.

That which is called "head" is not the "I." Likewise, the skin of the head is not called "I" either. The skull is only referred to as "skull," so it is not the "I." Similarly, being only eyes, the eyes are not the "I"; the ears, being only ears, are not the "I"; the nose, being naught but a nose, is not the "I"; and the tongue, being naught but a tongue, is not the "I." Teeth, being only teeth, are not the "I," nor is the brain; and all the muscles, blood, lymph, and veins are only ever referred to by their respective names. In this way, gain understanding!

The arm is but an arm, not the "I"; nor is the shoulder or shoulder blade. Neither the forearm nor the fingers are the "I" either. The spine is only a spine and not the "I"; the ribs are not the "I," nor the chest, nor the lungs, nor the heart. Moreover, the diaphragm is not the "I," nor the liver or spleen, nor the bowels or kidneys, nor the urine and feces. The marrow too is not referred to with the name "I." Furthermore, the thigh is simply called a "thigh," not "I. "The pelvis is likewise not the "I"; the hips are not the "I," nor is the lower leg or foot, and certainly not the toes.

In short, the outer skin is not called "I." The intermediate layers of muscle and fat are only known as muscle and fat, not as "I." The bones within are called bones and not named "I," and the innermost marrow is simply called marrow and not "I." Finally, even consciousness is called only that; it is not called "I." Therefore it is definitely emptiness, without any dweller or place where it might dwell.

In the same way, conclusively decide that this so-called I is totally beyond a place of departure or any being who might leave. Just like an optical illusion, it only appears to exist. Describing it is no different than describing a rabbit's horns.

Secondly, to establish the lack of self in things, there are four points:

1. Searching for the basis of labeling.
2. Abolishing the idea of matter being permanent.

3. Refuting the secret faults of benefit and harm.

4. Collapsing the falsehood of hope and fear.

First, if you look for the basis to which any name is attached, since no such basis exists, the name itself is empty— it is merely attached to projections of conceptual thoughts, for it is impossible to pinpoint the object of any label.

For example, what does the word "head" refer to and why? Is it because it grows first when the body forms? Or is it because it is round, or because it is found on top of the body? In fact, the head is not the first stage of the body's growth, everything round is not given the name "head," and, if one examines space, there is no above or below. Similarly, hair is not the head; skin is naught but skin and is not given the name "head." The skull is called "skull" alone; it is not named "head." The brain is not the head, nor are the eyes, ears, nose, or tongue.

You might now proclaim that separately these are not the head, only assembled together do they constitute a head. However, if you were to cut off the head of an animal, and pulverize it into particles, molecules, and atoms, then no matter to whom you showed it, no one in the entire world would call it a head. Even if the particles were mixed with water, such a mass would not be referred to as a head. Therefore know that the so-called head is nothing more than a verbal expression without objective basis

It goes the same for the eyes, for you don't call just any pair of viscous spheres "eyes"; the membrane is not the eye, nor are the viscous fluid or blood vessels the eyes. None of these individually or collectively can be called "the eyes." Even if the particles of these components were molded with water, you still wouldn't have a pair of eyes. The perceiver, being only a state of consciousness, is not the eyeballs. This is shown by the fact that one can see even during dreams and the bardo.

In the same way, the ear canals are not the ears, the skin is not the ears, nor are any of the flesh, veins, blood, or lymph the ears. The powder resulting from grinding all these to particles is not an ear, nor would it be if you added water and molded the mixture. If you think that the name ear is given to the one who hears sounds, then observe who hears sounds in dreams, during the waking state, and in the bardo. The one who hears is mind—the primordial consciousness—not the ear.

Similarly, the name "nose" is not given to nostrils, skin, bone, muscles, or veins, for they have their own names, none of which is "nose." The perceiver of odors is the consciousness itself, which is apparent if you examine what it is that perceives odors during dreams and in the bardo.

Moreover, if you analyze the tongue in the same way, the tissue, skin, blood, and veins all have their own names and individually are not called "tongue." The powder of the particles created by grinding them up is also not the tongue, nor is the result of mixing this powder with water and reshaping it called a tongue. The same reasoning applies to all of the following.

Concerning the arm, the shoulder is not the arm, nor is the upper arm, the forearm, the fingers, flesh, skin, bones, or marrow. Further, neither the skin, flesh, or bones is the shoulder; the collected particles are also not the shoulder, nor is the model made by mixing these with water. So the basis for the term "shoulder" is empty, as it has no real object.

When you analyze the upper arm and forearm in the same manner, each part has its own name—the flesh is called "flesh," bone is called "bone," skin is called "skin," and marrow is called "marrow"—thus there is not even the slightest objective basis for labeling.

By examining the foundation for the name "body" or "torso," the spine and ribs are not called "body." The chest, muscles, skin, and bones are not called "body." The heart, lungs, liver, midriff, spleen, kidneys, and entrails all have their own names as well. There is only emptiness; so, having no objective basis, the names "body" and "torso" are empty too.

By analyzing the leg in the same manner, you find that the hip is not the leg, nor is the thigh, the calf, or the foot. Similarly, the name "hip" is not given to muscle, nor to skin, bone, or veins. Nor is the word "thigh" given to skin, muscle, bone, or veins; the calf can be analyzed in the same way. Such terms apply neither to the powder created when these are ground into particles nor to the model made when this powder is mixed with water.

If you search for the basis of the word "mountain," earth is not a mountain and neither are grass, trees, stones, rocks, or rivers. Likewise, when searching for the basis of the term "house," just as the cement is not the house, neither is the stone or the wood. Walls are simply called "walls," not "house." Similarly, no basis whatsoever, inside or outside, can be found for the term "house."

Seeking the basis for names such as "human being," "horse," "dog," and so forth, you find that the eyes, ears, nose, tongue, flesh, blood, bones, marrow, and veins, as well as consciousness, have their own respective names and are not the objective basis for the names "man," "horse," "dog," and so on. Likewise, all things can be examined in this way.

For example, from among material objects, the name "drum" is not given to wood or hide, nor to the outside or inside. Similarly the steel is not called "knife," and the blade edge, the blade itself, the tip, and the handle also lack the object to which the name "knife" can be attached.

Furthermore, names also change according to function. For example, when a knife blade is ground down and becomes known as an awl, or when an awl is made into a needle, these former names all turn out to be objectless.

Based on the teachings given to me in the dream state by my guru, the noble and supreme Avalokiteshvara, I have thoroughly comprehended these two investigations into the so-called individual self and the basis to which names are attached.

Once when I envisioned the illusory wisdom form of Orgyen Tsokye Dorje,[11] he bestowed upon me instructions in the practice of recognizing all phenomena to be an illusion with these words: "In order to be introduced to the fact that all things are dependent upon the connection between cause and circumstance, consider the following:

"The causal basis is the transparent clarity of funda-

---

11. Guru Rinpoche or Padmasambhava.

mental space that has the capacity to let anything arise. The contributing circumstance is the ego-clinging consciousness. When these two come together, all phenomena manifest, just like illusions.

"Hence, basic space, the mind arising from its creative display, and all the outer and inner phenomena, which are the appearance aspect of that mind, are connected in a chain like the sun and its rays. Therefore it is called 'arising in interdependent connection.'

"A metaphor for this is when the transparent clarity of the sky—the causal basis—and the magician's props, mantras, and mind—the contributing circumstances—create a magical illusion—the dependent connection.

"In this way, all phenomena appear without existing, due to the power of clinging to the notion of self. This is like moisture and the vivid clarity of space coming together to create a mirage. As they appear without existing, to cling to all the apparent phenomena of waking consciousness, dreams, the bardo, and future lives is simply delusion—like grasping and clinging to solid objects during a dream without recognizing that it is a dream and that they are not real.

"Due to internally clinging to an 'I', the myriad objects and properties appear as something other, like a reflection appearing from the interdependent connection of a figure before a mirror.

"Due to being ensnared by our clinging to notions of self, the worlds of the six cities appear in random succession, like the appearance of a city of *gandharvas* on a plain at sunset. The various kinds of sights, sounds, smells, and sensations are subjective phenomena that only appear as other, like echoes. All appearances of sense objects are nonexistent from the beginning, like echoes.

"All appearing phenomena are of one taste in the fundamental nature and not separate from it, just as the reflections of planets and stars in the ocean are of one taste with the water and not separate from the ocean itself.

"Due to ego-clinging, self and other appear as real in the limitless expanse of the all-permeating fundamental space, like bubbles forming in water. Due to modifying the transparent clarity aspect of empty basic space so that it seems to be a solid self in the form of mental consciousness, all kinds of deluded phenomena appear. This is like the hallucinatory visions that appear when pressing on one's eyes or when one's nervous system is disturbed by an imbalance of subtle energies (*pranas*).

"Though from the viewpoint of the ego-clinging consciousness a great variety of things arise from our basic nature, they don't depart from or occur separately from the basic nature itself. This is similar to one who has mastered the samadhi of conjuring apparitions—when he enters that samadhi, all kinds of apparitions appear, but essentially they have no root or foundation and do not exist as real objects.

"Listen foolish little child! By progressively meditating in this way, you will realize that phenomena are illusions and you will become a yogi of illusion." And, upon saying this, he disappeared.

Having gained certainty in that way, I came to understand all phenomena to be empty in their very appearing. However, I still believed that sentient beings moved on to another realm, leaving behind the apparent external universe, the animate beings within, and all the desirable sense objects appearing in between. I also still thought that all beings possess individual natures.

Then I met my guru Longchenpa in a dream where he gave this pointing-out instruction in a dialectical form: "Listen noble son!" he said. "We fall asleep when the externally appearing universal vessel, the animate sentient beings contained within it, and the five kinds of sense objects appearing in between have all dissolved into the empty oblivion of the void of the all-ground, just like magical illusions melt into space. Then, due to movement of the karma prana, the magical display of the dream state unfolds including the vessel and its contents, sense objects, a self, a body, and related activity. If you cling to these as being real, you are deluded. Finally, the phenomena of this dream existence dissolve back into the empty blank space of the all-ground like a rainbow vanishing into the sky, and once again waking phenomena unfold as before."

To this I replied, "Though it is certain that my body is merely an appearance, doesn't it still arise from the causal and conditioning factors of my mother and father?"

"If you think that your body came from a mother and father," he asked, "then what do you think are the original origin, dwelling place, and final destination of the first father and mother?"

"I don't know, but they must exist," I said, "as I don't think it is possible to have a body without a mother and father."

"Then observe who the parents of the body are in dreams, in the bardo, and in the hell realms!" he said. Thereby, I concluded that this body merely appears to exist.

"Listen, kind lama," I continued, "having laid down in bed and pulled up the covers it seems to me that the dream phenomena arise while other people, the landscape, and so on, remain unchanged."

"The dream phenomena of the external appearance of the universal vessel is extremely vast," said the guru, "and the animate contents of sentient beings within it are beyond number, as are the beautifully displayed five kinds of sense objects appearing in between. Where, then, do all these dream phenomena unfold—inside the head, the limbs, or the upper or lower part of your body?"

Hence I concluded that this was not possible, so I said, "I believe that dream phenomena occur when the consciousness goes elsewhere; then when it reenters the body, waking phenomena arise again."

The guru replied, "If that is the case, then, since the body is apparently like a house, identify and describe to me the door of this house through which the consciousness comes and goes. Not only that, but you must also identify where the mind resides. If the mind resides in the upper part of the body, then why does one feel pain when pricked by a thorn in the lower part? Likewise, if the mind resides in the lower part, then there is no reason for feeling pain in the upper part.

"It is illogical to think that this subtle consciousness changes size, entering through a small opening, then expanding to pervade the body only to shrink again in order to exit through a tiny hole. If that were the case, then, when the body and mind separate at the time of death, why can this consciousness not reenter the body again?

"Also, where is this place you must go to see these dream phenomena? Above? Below? Or in any other direction?" he queried. "Do you believe that it is the same as the vessel of the universe and its contents during the waking state, or is it somewhere else? If you think it's the same, does sleep create a dividing line between them or not? If it does, then dream phenomena are not the same as waking phenomena; and if it doesn't, then there can be no such thing as dreams. Furthermore, there is no real benefit to believing that these phenomena are created and exist above or below, inside or outside."

To this I replied, "Guru, please, if this is so, then what conclusion should I draw? Sublime guru, please show me how I might find the answer."

To this request he said, "Throughout the beginningless succession of lives, no one has actually taken birth, but merely appeared to. Nor has anyone ever actually died; it was merely the transformation of phenomena like the shift from the dream state to the waking state. All experiences—seen, heard, smelled, tasted, and felt as forms, sounds, odors, tastes, and tactile sensations through the eyes, nose, ears, tongue, and skin—are merely self-arising phenomena appearing in and of themselves. Beyond that they don't even have as much as a tip of a hair's worth of existence.

"You may think that things are actually seen by the eye, grasped by the hand, or experienced through the sense doors and hence have a self-nature. However, though the forms, sounds, tastes, smells, and tactile sensations in dreams appear to be real at the time, when waking up it becomes clear that they never had any objective existence.

"Throughout a beginningless succession of samsaric lives, no one has ever actually shifted or moved from one place to another, nor has anyone ever stayed in some other place—this is merely like the occurrences in a dream.

"If you think that the authenticity of dream phenomena are not equal to those in the waking state, then ponder whether all the striving, efforts, and accumulations of riches in dreams and during the day, from the time you were born until now, are equal or not. When you minutely scrutinize the length of their duration and the size of their numbers, you will decide them to be equal.

"That is not all—if you believe dream phenomena to be unreal and waking phenomena to be real, then since dream phenomena are illusory and waking phenomena are not, you must then believe that dream phenomena are sentient beings and day phenomena enlightenment. And if both phenomena result from delusion, any distinction between true and false or real and unreal is meaningless, because 'deluded phenomena' implies believing that something exists when it doesn't.

"In the past we have eaten a quantity of food equal to the size of Mount Meru and have drunk oceans to quench our thirst, but still we have not been filled. Though we have worn as much cloth as there is in the three thousand-fold universe, we are still not warm. Understand that these examples are indications that none of these possess any existence, but are mere appearances.

"It is a major flaw not to understand that this corporeal appearance is empty, and instead to believe it to be real. Because the great efforts we go to for the sake of this body consume the fruit of omniscience, clinging to the body as being real is known as the devouring demon. Since it chains together an endless succession of samsaric existences and causes birth and death to appear, it is 'the funeral parade.' As it forces you to strive for happiness through good clothing and the like, thus severing the aorta of liberation with the hope and fear perpetuated by clinging to attachment and aversion, it is known as 'the executioner.' Since it robs one of the breath of lasting happiness, it is also called 'the vital breath–stealer.'

"Therefore, all those who cling to apparent objects of the six gatherings[12] are like a deer mistaking a mirage to be water and running after it, for beyond the appearance, such phenomena don't possess the least iota of existence.

"Though you might understand that things are empty in this way, they remain seemingly real as before and do not disappear, leading you to wonder what use there is in acquiring such knowledge. If you do not realize that emptiness is the essence of meditation, then all your attempts to meditate will surely fall into indifference or apathy."

He continued, "You might also wonder that since the mere intellectual understanding obtained through all the other conceptual forms of meditation won't liberate you, why would merely realizing emptiness necessarily lead to revealing the basic nonexistence of things as well, leading you to

---

12. These are the six senses; the six aggregates of consciousness.

think that if everything is already empty, then it makes no difference whether one knows it or not. However, samsara and nirvana, freedom and delusion, originate from the difference between awareness and unawareness, knowing and not knowing. So to know and to be aware of it should be understood to be a crucial point.

"Furthermore, some people say that if you can't figure this out on your own, study and contemplation are useless. Yet, since beginningless time, you have not realized this on your own and so have been wandering in samsara. So take heed, by practice and study one will realize the view of emptiness in accordance with all the tantras, scriptures, and instructions!

"Moreover, the result is the same whether you realize emptiness after having undergone great hardships, such as practice and study, or if you do so without engaging in the slightest effort, just as, for example, there is no difference in the quality of gold whether it is found after great hardship or under your bed without any effort at all.

"This analyzing knowledge that establishes all phenomena to be emptiness is called discerning intelligence. The continuing knowledge, which uninterruptedly definitively decides samsara and nirvana to be the great emptiness, is called the intelligence realizing egolessness. When these two kinds of intelligence have taken birth in one's nature, it is a crucial point, first to understand, then to experience, and finally to attain conviction.

"Still you may persist, saying that it is unreasonable to believe that the body and so forth do not exist beyond mere appearances, because an individual who has realized the empty nature of his or her body still feels pain when the body is touched by water or fire, or is struck by an arrow, spear, or stick. However, until one has arrived at the basic space of exhaustion in dharmata, dualistic phenomena will not disappear. And as long as they have not disappeared, beneficial and harmful appearances will occur uninterruptedly. This is shown when the body remains unburned even in the midst of the flames of hell.

Upon saying this, he disappeared.

Another time, when I met the great siddha Saraha, I asked him, "Mighty lord of siddhas, what are obscurations and how can I purify myself of them? What exactly is the deity that I am to accomplish? What demons and obstacles must I beware of, and how can I free myself of them? Please explain all this to me."

In response, he bestowed these words: "Listen, great being! You must attack the lair of benefit and harm. The terms *obscuration* and *ignorance* refer to being unaware of the essential nature of fundamental emptiness. When obscurations and ignorance become entrenched, they are known as habitual habits. These cannot be purified by ordinary efforts, such as exerting oneself in virtuous actions of body and speech. Rather, by attaining conviction about the nature of all things, they will naturally become purified through discerning intelligence.

"Where do all the beneficial virtuous karmas of body and speech abide? Where is the storehouse in which they are accumulated? By investigating where they come from, where they abide, and where they go to, no such place is found to exist, so of what benefit can they be?

"Investigate: Where is the benefit—in the outside, inside, middle, top, or bottom of the empty nature of mind? Discovering it to be intangible, you must conclude that the virtuous karmas of body and speech amount to nothing more than accumulated merit of samsara!

"Similarly, ask yourself, where is the accumulated heap of nonvirtue? Where is its storehouse located? And what does it harm in the outside, inside, top, bottom, or middle of the empty mind?

"When you closely scrutinize the mindstreams of those who constantly engage in virtuous acts of body and speech and compare them to those who have practiced nonvirtue their entire lives, you will see that there isn't even the slightest difference between their perpetuation of attachment and aversion, hope and fear. When liberated, they are free because their mindstreams are freed. When deluded, they are deluded because their mindstreams are deluded. So as long as one's mindstream is not liberated, there isn't the slightest difference in respect to wandering in samsara. Therefore, when not transcended, the only difference between virtue and nonvirtue is the creation of temporary happiness and suffering, in addition to which both only perpetuate samsara.

"If, during the process of gaining certainty about virtue, you confuse the path of complete liberation with the virtue of accumulating temporary merit, then you will not attain the goal of omniscience. And if, while ascertaining nonvirtue, you don't recognize that obscuration and the ground of delusion are not being aware of your true nature, then you will fail to identify the cause of delusion. If that happens, you will only perpetuate confusion and roam endlessly in samsara. Hence, understand that it is crucial to gain certainty in regard to virtue and nonvirtue.

"When you analyze the original source, the dwelling place, and finally the place of disappearance of all the so-called helpful and protective gods, no such locations can be found. In which of the forms, sounds, smells, tastes, and tactile sensations that manifest in the sense fields do these gods exist? If you think they can be found in any of the elements, particles, or atoms that comprise the universe, then examine the respective names and substances of those elements. By minutely examining how these gods could be of benefit and, similarly, how demons could cause harm, you will conclude that they are intangible and nowhere to be found. Every joy and sorrow is merely a mental experience appearing as if in a dream. Other than that, there is nothing that could be objectively referred to as helpful gods or harmful demons.

"If you believe that demons inflict harm, when you analyze how they do so, you will discover that the effect of these so-called demons extends no further than the word 'harm,' since they are not found among the objects of form, sound, odor, taste, or tactile sensation. They are empty, intangible, and have no objective existence.

"Under the influence of delusion, people regard the upper and lower parts of their bodies to be good and bad, respectively, as the upper torso appears to be clean, like they would consider a god to be, and the lower part of the body appears to be dirty, like they imagine a demon would be. Due to holding such opinions, hope and fear arise unceasingly.

"Due to the tight chains of clinging to the notion of a self, sensations of pleasure and pain appear uninterruptedly, yet all these are only ephemeral experiences of samsara, beyond which they don't possess even the slightest actual existence. This is clearly demonstrated by the metaphor of a dream. Knowing that this is how things actually are dispels the obstacles to meditation.

"When all the hindrances due to not relying on or trusting in meditation have been dispelled, you will gain a steadfast conviction in the true nature of all things, which is free of all doubt. In addition, freed from the veil of unawareness, you will attain mastery of the great, vast, continuous nature of awareness.

"This is also the root meaning of the profound teachings of pacifying and cutting through demons. Decide that there is no deity to seek other than your own intrinsic awareness and no demons other than conceptual thoughts. This knowledge is indispensable to all practices for accomplishing deities and all ceremonies for expelling demons. Knowing this, you are sure to be a great yogic master of illusion, one who realizes that all phenomena are illusory.

"Listen, mindless little awareness child![13] You should teach this to all your disciples and they too will become yogis of the Great Vehicle of the Definitive Secret."

---

13. "Mindless" is used in the sense of having transcended conceptual thoughts and dualistic mind.

Upon saying this, he vanished.

Another time while beholding the countenance of the great and majestic Vajrapani in a pure vision of luminous clarity, I asked the following: "Please, great vajra-holding buddha, does 'awakening' imply awakening here unto oneself or does one go some other place to awaken?"

"Listen, fortunate and noble son!" he answered. "Perhaps you think that a buddha is someone of royalty who is captivating to behold, peaceful and calm, with a flawless complexion and peerless beauty, living in a vast spacious country. If so, then who are his parents? If he is born from a mother, is he limited to being produced? If he abides somewhere, is he limited to permanence? If he ceases and disappears, is he limited to nothingness? In short, if there is an essential nature that can be established to truly exist yet which is subject to arising, abiding, and ceasing, then there can be no natural state that is free from the two extremes. So any phenomena that appear to arise and cease are merely the result of conceptual labeling.

"If you insist that what belongs to complete and perfect enlightenment has objective existence, you will be tied by your own rope. If there is any difference between the nature of samsara and that of nirvana, then any reference to the oneness of samsaric existence and the peaceful state of nirvana would be nothing but empty talk. Many, indeed, cling to nirvana as having its own separate existence and hence become ensnared by hope and fear.

"If you perceive differences in the vast array of enjoyments, riches, and ornaments of the buddha fields and believe them to possess substantial existence, it is called 'clinging to the self of phenomena.'

"To regard a tathagata as possessing a constant and real existence, no matter what you call it, is nothing more than the view of an individual self. If you think that a buddha has eyes, then he must also have visual consciousness; and once there is visual consciousness, then the appearance of visual forms is inevitable. When these perceived visual objects come into being, the arising of subtle mental grasping cannot be avoided, and this is called 'the mental attachment of vision.' That which conceives the duality of grasper and grasped is called mind, hence anything possessing such a mind is called a 'sentient being.'

"Likewise, if you think that a buddha has ears, he must also have auditory consciousness with its attendant sounds. If you think he has a nose, then he must also have an olfactory consciousness together with smells. If he has a tongue, he must also have taste consciousness together with tastes, and if you think he possesses a body, then he must also have tactile consciousness together with tactile sensations. These comprise the various objects of grasping. The conceptual thoughts that grasp them are the various perceptual faculties of the mind, and, as before, that which possesses mind is called a sentient being. Even if it were possible for a buddha who is not beyond the duality of perceptual subject and object to exist, a sentient being who assumed the characteristics of such a buddha would still remain just an ordinary human being.

"You might think that a buddha teaches the Dharma

to others, and in doing so views himself as a teacher, the Dharma as something to be taught, and sentient beings as the recipients of the teachings. But such a person wouldn't have a sesame seed's worth of superior characteristics to that of a sentient being and would be a sentient being himself.

"If you believe that the special qualities of a buddha are residing in a pleasant place, having physical beauty, excellent companions, great wealth, and happiness, while being free of anger and attachment, then you are still describing a sentient being who is no more superior than a god in the form realm.

"In actual fact, your own fundamental nature, Samantabhadra, is what is meant by 'the sugata of the three times.'

"From the perspective of the ultimate truth, no buddha has ever appeared in the world or ever taught the Dharma. Many tantras, scriptures, and instructions clearly explain how the teacher appears to the disciple as his or her own self-arising phenomena; so refer to those texts to clarify this matter.

"Moreover, if you believe that other samsaric realms exist, where many sentient beings go and transmigrate, experiencing happiness and suffering, that too is illogical. If it is true that one's previous body appears to be left behind, where does the body of the bardo state come from? When sentient beings in our present life can die merely by getting wounded, receiving a burn on their arms or legs, or from the extreme cold of a single winter's day, how is it that when one has obtained a body that experiences heat and cold in the hell realms, it does not perish even though it is boiled and burned for long periods? Similarly, when we can die from starvation in just a matter of days or months, why don't the *preta* beings die though they suffer starvation for aeons? For this reason, all the six classes of sentient beings, including those in the bardo, are deluded, because they become attached to a reality that does not exist, being nothing more than a mere appearance that is empty and insubstantial, just like the phenomena of a dream.

"When, in this way, you have established the nature of the phenomena that arise from delusion and understood them to be unreal, empty, and insubstantial, you will have emptied the depths of samsara. When you have resolved that there is no buddha other than your own inherent nature and have gained confidence, you will have actually attained what is referred to as 'the self-liberation of countless buddhas.'

"Listen, mighty expanse of sky, all-pervading vajra, you must establish that all phenomena in samsara and nirvana are utterly empty and so realize their inherent nature to be non-existence."

Upon saying this, he disappeared.

After analyzing like this for a long time, I gained an unshakeable conviction regarding nonexistence. But, though I knew all the apparent phenomena of the universe and its contents to be empty in themselves, the emptiness aspect became overemphasized and I became indifferent. At this point, I happened to meet Chemchok Dorje Drolö singing the song of HUNG, which reveals samsara and nirvana to be the play of emptiness.[14]

"Please, most excellent divinity, Great Supreme One," I

---

14. Chemchok Dorje Drolö is a wrathful emanation of Guru Rinpoche.

beseeched him, "though I understand that samsara and nirvana are emptiness, this emptiness remains neither beneficial nor harmful. Do you have any advice in this regard?"

"Listen, you mighty expanse of sky!" the deity replied. "You should determine all of samsara and nirvana to be emptiness, determine emptiness to be the essential nature, determine this essential nature to be the basic ground, determine samsara and nirvana to be the display of this basic ground, and determine the common denominator of both samsara and nirvana to be none other than this basic ground itself.

"The reflections of the stars and planets in the ocean are the display of the ocean itself. Space is the matrix of the universe and its contents. Dharma nature pervades all of samsara and nirvana. Ponder the meaning of these examples and you will become a yogi who instantaneously perfects samsara and nirvana."

Saying this, he disappeared.

Seven years later, I met the dharmakaya teacher Vajradhara in a pure vision and implored him, "Please, teacher and transcendent perfect conqueror, explain how one is freed on the path of liberation and omniscience, and how one is deluded on the profane path of samsara."

Hearing my request he replied, "Listen here, great being! Buddhas and sentient beings differ due to awareness and unawareness. The basic ground, the primordial buddha Samantabhadra, is characterized by the four kayas and five wisdoms.

"The empty essence is dharmakaya, the cognizant nature is sambhogakaya, the self-liberating manifest capacity is nirmanakaya, and its pervasiveness throughout all of samsara and nirvana is *svabhavikakaya*.

"Everything takes place within the openness of this basic ground, so it is the all-encompassing space known as dharmadhatu. Since it is an untainted vivid clarity, it is like a mirror. As its displays of samsara and nirvana are of equal purity, it is equality. In it, the apperceptions of knowing and perceiving are unobstructed, so it is discerning. And because it performs all actions in purity and freedom, it is all-accomplishing.

"The path awareness that liberates within self-existing buddhahood also actualizes the four kayas and five wisdoms present in the essential nature. The essence of awareness is all-pervading, like the continuum of space, insubstantial, inexpressible, a vast transparent clarity, a playground that is rootless and groundless and totally unelaborate, therefore it is the dharmakaya. As the nature of this awareness is naturally cognizant, it is sambhogakaya. Since the expression of its cognizant nature is unobstructed, it is nirmanakaya. Being the common ground of samsara and nirvana, it is svabhavikakaya.

"Having established the view of the ground, to see that samsara and nirvana are of one taste in the basic space of reality is the dharmadhatu wisdom. Not allowing emptiness to become a mindless void, but rather letting it remain a vivid, immaculate lucidity—like a spotless mirror in which anything can appear—is the mirror-like wisdom. To know that the qualities of samsara and nirvana are equal in the supreme emptiness is the wisdom of equality. To realize the expression of awareness as the unobstructed lucidity of distinctly perceiving intelligence is discerning wisdom. When awareness masters itself, the activities of both purifying and freeing are naturally perfected, which is the action of all-accomplishing wisdom.

"Many people, not familiar with the modes of this path of awareness just-as-it-is, take as path a passive state in which mind and awareness have not been distinguished. They are unclear about external phenomena, which they grasp at as having substance and self-existence. While inwardly they are unclear about their own body, chained to holding it to be permanent and real, they are completely gagged and bound. Even though they may attain stability in a state of unobstructed, lucid consciousness situated somewhere between these two poles, apart from creating the merit to be born in the two higher realms, they will not attain a state of liberation and omniscience and are therefore not flawless.

"Understanding that all phenomena within samsara and nirvana are of one taste in the nature of suchness (*dharmata*), just as it is, is the intelligence of knowing things as they are. When abiding in the state of awareness, the unimpeded, self-existing, all-cognizing consciousness is the intelligence of knowing all that there is. Although this awareness is unimpeded, just like a drop of mercury falling on the ground, it does not get entangled with objects.

"The mind regards samsara and nirvana as having independent natures, it views appearances as substantial entities, and it is unaware of the actual nature of the basic ground. In this mind, thoughts come and go and become entangled with objects, like a drop of water falling on dry earth.

"When the true face of the pure fundamental buddha, who is master of the basic ground, was obscured by unawareness, all the kayas and wisdoms that comprise the natural luminosity of the basic ground dissolved into this inner radiance. This radiance shifted outwardly to external radiance, in the form of five-colored light that unfolded as the play of the five elements in the following manner.

"When the dharmadhatu wisdom was obscured by unawareness, the external radiance appears as blue light; this is the essence of space that is called the inner or major element. However, with the belief that it is real, attachment to this light as a substance develops, and it appears as an impure phenomenon: the external or minor element known as space.

"When the mirror-like wisdom was obscured by unawareness and dissolves into the inner radiance, the external radiance appears as white light. This light is the inner or major element known as the essence of water. However, with the belief that it is real, attachment to this light as a substance develops, and it appears as an impure phenomenon: the external or minor element known as water.

"When the equality wisdom was obscured by unawareness and dissolves into the inner radiance, the external radiance appears as yellow light. This light is the inner or major element known as the essence of earth. However, with the belief that it is real, attachment to this light as a substance develops, and it appears as an impure phenomenon: the external or minor element known as earth.

"When the discerning wisdom was obscured by unaware-ness and dissolves into inner radiance, the external radiance appears as red light. This light is the inner or major element known as the essence of fire. However, with the belief that it is real, attachment to this light as a substance develops, and it appears as an impure phenomenon: the external or minor element known as fire.

"When the all-accomplishing wisdom was obscured by unawareness and dissolves into inner radiance, the exter-nal radiance appears as green light. This light is the inner or major element known as the essence of wind. However, with the belief that it is real, attachment to this light as a sub-stance develops, and it appears as an impure phenomenon: the external or minor element known as wind.

"Due to the luminosity of these five lights, phenomena of various colors and of the five elements appear uninter-ruptedly.

"The way in which the five basic delusions arise from the function of these obscured wisdoms is as follows: When the basic ground is obscured by unawareness, it becomes the all-ground with attributes, which is a blank void like space where nothing perceives or appears. It is similar to the state of deep sleep or the loss of consciousness upon fainting. To become dispersed in this state is the nature of stupidity, the vast fog of unawareness. In this state the karma prana of the *kalpa* stirs; this is the nature of envy. The functioning of this karma prana causes clarity to emerge from the emptiness; this is the all-ground consciousness, which abides as the nature of anger. From this comes the clinging to the mere feeling of self as 'I'; this is the defiled mental consciousness, which abides as the nature of pride. From this, the mental faculty arises, which constitutes the ability for phenomena to appear in the blank void of the basic ground and which brings forth an aspect of lucidity. This abides as the nature of desire.

"All five of these natures arise from the internal radiance as external radiance. The nature of these five poisons spits out a horde of afflicted thoughts, like sparks from a fire.

"Thus, appearances unfold in the field of unobstructed space provided by the empty cognizance pervading both the all-ground and the mental faculty equally. When the condition—the stirring of the karma prana—meets with the cause—the all-ground endowed with the potential for allowing things to arise—then various kinds of visual forms appear in such a manner that they are based on this ground and connected to it, being nothing other than this ground itself. This field where visual appearances take shape is conventionally called 'eye consciousness' or 'vision.'

"Therefore, the field for appearances, which is likened to an ocean, is known as the 'object' or 'field.' Any visual appearance, which can be likened to the stars and planets reflected in the ocean, is known as 'the grasped.' Then the grasper—the subtle mental faculty—labels these visual forms, grasps them as objects, and regards them as substantial entities. The resultant conceptual thinking that takes forms to be pleasant, painful, or indifferent is called 'the visual grasping mind.'

"Similarly, the unobstructed field where sound appears

is the field, and the apparent sounds that manifest are 'the grasped objects', and the grasping mental consciousness is 'the auditory grasping mind.' As above, there is an interdependent connection of cause and circumstance.

"Similarly, phenomena in the form of smells, tastes, and tactile sensations are conventionally known as the olfactory consciousness, taste consciousness, and tactile consciousness, respectively. However, as demonstrated by their arising in dreams and the bardo, they do not enter through the individual openings of the senses.

"Some people believe that appearances are mind, wondering whether all external phenomena are actually conceptual thoughts and thus their own minds. This, however, is not the case, because all phenomena change from the very moment they appear, gradually ceasing and fading away. So it is taught that even though appearances rise and fall in the mind, they are not the mind.

"When phenomena of the eight aggregates progressively emerge in the given order, samsara unfolds in its entirety.[15] When the order is reversed, down to the all-ground consciousness, this is called being 'wearied at the peak of existence.'

"Thus, being no other than the basic ground itself, all apparent phenomena and existence, the whole of samsara and nirvana, are of one taste with it. As an example, take the

15. The eight aggregates are the eight collections of consciousness: the all-ground consciousness, the defiled mental consciousness, the mental cognition, and the cognitions of eye, ear, nose, tongue, and body.

countless reflections of the planets and stars, which, though they appear in the ocean, are actually of one taste with the water itself. Understand that this is how it is.

"This is Vajradhara's teaching describing how all appearances are self-phenomena."

Upon saying this, he disappeared.

The Essence of Wakefulness

A Method in Sustaining the Nature of Awareness

Mipham Rinpoche

Homage to the glorious Primordial Protector.

When you practice sustaining the nature of awareness, the three stages of recognizing, training, and attaining stability will gradually occur.

First of all, scrutinize the naked and natural face of awareness by means of your master's oral instructions until you are able to see it free from assumptions.

Having resolved it with certainty, it is essential that you simply sustain the nature of just that. It is not enough merely to recognize it—you must perfect the training in the following way:

You may already have recognized the face of awareness, but unless you rest in just that, conceptual thinking will interrupt it and it will be difficult for awareness to appear nakedly. So, at that point, it is essential to rest without accepting or rejecting your thoughts and to continue by repeatedly resting in the state of unfabricated awareness.

When you have practiced this again and again, the force of your thought waves weakens, while the face of your awareness grows sharper and becomes easier to sustain.

That is when you should abide in the meditation state as much as you can and be mindful of remembering the face of awareness during post-meditation. As you grow used to this, the strength of your awareness increases.

At first, when a thought occurs, you need not apply a remedy to stop it. By leaving it to itself, at some point it is freed naturally—just as the knot on a snake unties itself.

When you become more adept, the occurrence of a thought will cause slight turmoil but immediately vanish in itself—just like a drawing on the surface of water.

When you train in that, you gain experience that transcends benefit and harm, at which point thought occurrences cause no problem whatsoever. Thus, you will be free from hope or fear about whether or not thoughts do occur—just like a thief entering an uninhabited house.

By practicing further, you perfect the training so that, finally, your conceptual thinking and the all-ground, along with its impetus, dissolve into unfabricated dharmakaya. That is the attainment of the natural abode of awareness.

Just as you cannot find any ordinary stones on an island of gold even if you search for them, all that appears and exists will be experienced as the realm of dharmakaya. Attaining stability is when everything has become all-encompassing purity.

Likewise, just as conceptual thinking gradually declines under the power of awareness during the daytime, at night you do not need to apply some other instruction, but should simply understand how the recognition of dreams and the luminosities of shallow and deep sleep correspond.

Until you attain stability, by all means continue with undistracted diligence, like the steady flow of a river.

This was taught by Mipham. May virtuous goodness increase.

Nyoshul Khen Rinpoche

THE MIRROR OF MINDFULNESS

Nyoshul Khen Rinpoche

Homage to the king of self-existing mindfulness.

Look here, all vajra friends!

I am the vajra of mindfulness. When seeing me be
mindful!

Look into the essence of the immovable mind!

I am the mirror of mindfulness clearly showing your
mindful attention.

Mindfulness is the root of Dharma.

Mindfulness is the main part of the practice.

Mindfulness is the stronghold of the mind.

Mindfulness is the aid to spontaneously aware wisdom.

Without mindfulness one is carried away by laziness.

A lack of mindfulness is the creator of all faults.

A lack of mindfulness doesn't accomplish any purpose.

A lack of mindfulness is like a heap of excrement.

To lack mindfulness is to sleep in an ocean of urine.

To lack mindfulness is to be like a heartless corpse.

Friends, please be mindful!
Through the aspiration of the supreme guru, may all
friends attain firm mindfulness!

*These words urging one to be mindful were composed by the stupid,
bucktoothed ox, the bad monk, Jamyang Dorje, and offered to his vajra
friends. May it be virtuous!*

THE LAMP
THAT DISPELS DARKNESS

An Instruction that Points Directly to the Nature
of Mind in the Tradition of the Old Realized Ones

Mipham Rinpoche

Homage to the guru and Manjushri Jnanasattva.

Without having to study, reflect, and train extensively,
But by maintaining mind-essence through the tradition
of oral instruction,
An ordinary town yogi can, with minor hardship, arrive
at the vidyadhara level;
This is the power of the profound path.

When your attention is allowed to settle naturally without thinking of anything and you maintain constant mindfulness in that state, you experience a neutral and indifferent state of mind that is vacant and blank. As long as an insight of decisive knowing is not present, this is exactly what masters call unknowing (*ma rigpa*). You cannot define it with phrases like "it's like this" or "this is it"—so such a state of mind is also called undecided (*lungmaten*). And, unable to say where you remain or what you are thinking of, this state is labeled common indifference (*thamal tang-nyom*). In fact, you have slipped into the ordinary common state of the all-ground.

Nonconceptual wakefulness should be developed through this method of settling. However, as it lacks a wakefulness that knows your own nature, it is not the main meditation training. This is what the "Aspiration of Samantabhadra" says:

> *The vacant state of not thinking of anything*
> *Is itself the cause of ignorance and confusion.*

Since your mind does experience this vacant state, which lacks both thought and mental activity, look naturally into the one who notices this state, the one who is not thinking. When you do so, there is a thought-free knowing (rigpa) that is totally open, free from inside and outside, like a clear sky.[16] This knowing is not a duality of that experienced and that experiencing, but you can resolve that it is your own nature and feel the conviction that "it is no other than this." As this state cannot be expressed precisely with concepts or descriptions, once you feel such conviction, it can appropriately be described as beyond extremes, indescribable, innate luminosity, awareness, or knowing (rigpa).

---

16. In this text, *rigpa* is translated as "knowing," so as to follow simple explanations by Tulku Urgyen Rinpoche and Nyoshul Khen Rinpoche.

Then the wakefulness of knowing your nature will dawn, the obscurity of the vacuous state will be cleared, and, just as the interior of a house becomes visible with the rising of the sun, you will find certainty in the nature of your mind. This is the instruction in breaking open the eggshell of ignorance.

With that realization, you will understand that the basic and timeless presence of such a nature is not formed out of causes and conditions, that it does not change throughout the three times, and that, separate from this nature, the existence of some other thing called "mind" cannot be found, not even so much as an atom.

Although the previous vacant state was indescribable, unable to describe it, you failed to clearly resolve it. The identity of knowing is also indescribable, but you will have now resolved this fact beyond any doubt, and so there is a great difference in the ineffability of each, much like the difference between having eyesight and being blind.

This also explains the essential distinction between the all-ground and dharmakaya.

Similarly, terms such as ordinary mind, mental nondoing, ineffability, and so on, can indicate both appropriate and inappropriate states. So when you comprehend this crucial point of "similar word but exalted meaning," you can experience and realize the profound Dharma.

When about to settle in the natural way of mind-essence, some people merely try to stay conscious and aware and then rest in the state of mind consciousness with the feeling, "Ah, how clear!" Other people fixate on a state of utter void as if their mind had gone blank. Both of these cases, however, are merely aspects of mind consciousness clinging to a dualistic experience. Whenever this happens—when there is both clarity and one perceiving clarity, or emptiness and one perceiving emptiness—look into the nature of this stream of rigidly fixated mindfulness. By doing so, you pull up the stake to which is tied the dualistic mind that maintains a perceiver and something perceived, and you disentangle the naked and wide-open natural state—a luminous emptiness without center or edge.

To resolve this bright and open natural state is called the essence of knowing; it is the dawn of the naked wakefulness of knowing free from the covers of fixated experience. This is the instruction in cutting through the web of samsaric existence.

With this spontaneous self-cognizance of your innate nature, recognize the knowing that is free from the various covers of assumptions and temporary experiences—just as rice is free from its husk. Merely recognizing this nature of knowing however is not enough; you must stabilize a steady familiarity with this state. So it is important to sustain, without distraction, a constant remembrance of settling into the natural state.

As you continue to practice in this way, sometimes there may be a dull and absentminded state of unknowing. Sometimes there may be a thought-free state of openness revealing vipashyana's brilliance. Sometimes there may be an experience of bliss with attachment, sometimes an experience of bliss without attachment. Sometimes there may be various experiences of clarity with fixation, sometimes a flawless brilliance free from fixation. Sometimes there may be unpleasant and grueling experiences, sometimes pleasant and smooth experiences. Sometimes there may be a strong turbulence of discursive thought that carries you away and disperses the meditation, sometimes a torpid state of dullness without any clarity.

These and other types of unpredictable experiences are thought states cultivated since beginningless time, the countless waves of the karmic wind. They are like the varying pleasant or precipitous scenery during a long journey. Therefore, maintain the natural state without attaching any special importance to whatever arises.

Not yet having fully trained in this practice, don't become discouraged by any experiences of turbulence in which a multitude of thoughts blaze up like a fire. Instead, maintain unbroken practice by keeping a balance between tight and loose. By doing so, the experiences of attainment, and so on, will gradually occur. Usually, at this point, you will gain confidence in the difference between knowing and unknowing, all-ground and dharmakaya, consciousness and wakefulness, as recognized in your own experience through the oral instructions of the guru.

When maintaining this recognition—like water, which clears when left undisturbed—let your consciousness settle in itself as its nature of wakefulness is naturally present. This instruction should be regarded as the chief point.

Don't get involved in speculations about what to accept or reject, such as, "Is my meditation object consciousness or wakefulness?" Neither should you rely on theoretical book knowledge, which only increases thought activity. These involvements may obscure your shamatha and vipashyana.

At some point, you will reach a more stable familiarity with shamatha and vipashyana as a natural unity—shamatha being an ongoing steadiness in remembering to settle in the natural state, and vipashyana the recognizing of your essence as natural cognizance. Attaining this stability, in which the shamatha of primordially abiding in the natural state and the vipashyana of natural luminosity are basically indivisible, is the dawn of self-existing wakefulness, the realization of dzogchen. This is the instruction for abiding in space-like equanimity.

The glorious Saraha said:

> *Completely abandoning the thinker and what is thought of,*
> *Remain like a thought-free child.*

This is the method of resting, and

> *if you apply yourself to the guru's words and endeavor,*
> *when you have obtained the instruction that brings you face*
> *to face with knowing (rigpa),*
> *the coemergent will dawn without a doubt.*

Thus dawns the self-existing wakefulness that is rigpa— the nature of your mind, which is primordially coemergent with your mind. This nature (*dharmata*) of all things (*dharmas*) is also the original and ultimate luminosity.

This being so, settling in naturalness and sustaining the rigpa of recognizing one's natural face, the mind-essence or nature of mind, is an instruction that condenses a hundred vital points into one. Moreover, this is what you should sustain continuously.

Mark the degree of progress in this practice by the strength of the luminosity at night. Understand that the signs for being on the correct path are a spontaneous increase in faith, compassion, and intelligence. Experience within yourself the ease of this practice and the lessening of hardship. Be certain of its depth and swiftness, for your realization is no different from that produced with the greatest effort on other paths.

The fruition to be attained by training in your mind's luminous wakefulness is that, as the obscuration of thoughts and habitual tendencies naturally clears (*sang*) and the twofold knowledge effortlessly unfolds (*gye*),[17] you will capture the primordial kingdom and spontaneously accomplish the three kayas.

PROFOUND. GUHYA. SAMAYA.

On the auspicious twelfth day of the second month in the year of the Fire Horse (April 6, 1906), Mipham Jampal Dorje wrote this practical guidance with comprehensible Dharma terms, a profound instruction in accord with the experience of all the old realized ones, for the benefit of town yogis who do not especially wish to exert themselves in general studies and reflections, yet still desire to train in mind-essence.

May it be virtuous.

---

17. *Sangye* is Tibetan for Buddha

OLD VIJAYA

Shechen Gyaltsab, Pema Namgyal

Homage to the guru.

Here is advice to the devoted and sincere Riksang who is of noble family.

If you want your Dharma practice to be genuine, make sure first of all that the topics of the hard-to-achieve freedoms and riches, death and impermanence, the consequences of actions, and the defects of samsara do not become mere words and ideas, but reflect upon them from the core of your heart. So that once you are well acquainted with them, your mind will have turned away from the entirety of samsara's luxuries and—as a matter of course—you will only be interested in the sublime Dharma, so that nothing else matters. Once you feel this way, you have already covered half of Dharma practice.

In addition to that, keep reminding yourself of the excellent qualities of your guru and the Three Jewels. Having trained in this, you will seek no other refuge than your guru and the Three Jewels, no matter what joys or sorrows befall you. Once that happens, you will have become one of the Buddha's followers. That itself is the refuge training, the foundation for all other precepts.

In addition to that, train in accepting all sentient beings as your parents, and, maintaining this attitude uninterruptedly, cultivate loving-kindness, compassion, and awakened mind. Once you have become accustomed to this, you are capable of benefitting others in whatever you do and you are forever free of the chain of selfishness. When that has happened, you are included among the Mahayana followers, and this is how you deserve the name "child of the conquerors." The merit and benefits of this are beyond measure.

These are the ways in which you avoid going astray from the true path. So, as long as you have not yet succeeded in the above, it does not matter at all how well you can chant or do a sadhana, how lofty your view is or deep your meditation, or how meticulous your behavior is, because everything you do becomes nothing other than seeking worldly goals and pursuing food and clothing. This does not bring you even a millimeter closer to the true path. You have simply fooled yourself and become your own deceiver. Since this is so, do your utmost to instead take those topics to heart.

To be a Dharma person, you must integrate the teachings into your heart. Practice should mean that your efforts act as an effective remedy against the three poisons. A Dharma practice that does not remedy selfish emotions is completely useless. The Dharma has taken birth in your being when your mind fuses with the teachings such that the teachings remedy ego-clinging. Your Dharma has now become the path; it has been successful.

From then on, whichever practice you do related to the four empowerments—whether it be development stage, recitation, or completion stage with or without concepts—it will now genuinely be the unexcelled, swift path, and it will not lead down a wrong track.

The perspective of development stage is to acknowledge that all phenomena—the multitude of thoughts and concepts that comprise aggregates, elements, and sense bases—from the beginning possess a nature of "cleared perfection." As a deity mandala of the three bases of completeness, all phenomena are undivided purity and equality. It is while acknowledging this that the three aspects of vivid features, pure symbolism, and stable pride are of utmost importance, as are the three of purifying, perfecting, and maturing. If you lack this vital point of acknowledgment and instead regard a deity as having a real material face with eyes and a nose, I cannot guarantee where you will end up.

As to reciting and chanting, you should do them while acknowledging that since the beginning the movements of breath and energies, as well as all voices and sounds of the animate and inanimate world, are the utterly perfect speech of the conquerors, the never-arising audible emptiness. It is while acknowledging this that you should possess the vital points of recitation, such as the four nails that bind the life-force. If you lack this vital point of acknowledgment, but instead absentmindedly recite with roving gaze and unbridled tongue, just flapping your lips up and down, it is not likely to yield a profound result.

Now, the completion stage is to recognize that your basic nature is the awakened mind of knowing, beyond bondage and liberation, the vajra mind of the conquerors since the beginning. Do not allow your recognizing this to be just an assumption or pretense, but recognize the true natural state of your mind, without being mistaken. It is while knowing this that you should keep recognizing, like the steady flow of a great river, instead of picking or choosing, accepting or rejecting. Otherwise, concentrating obsessively, being over-ambitious, or continuing with the hollowness of theories and generalizations will get you nowhere.

In order to truly recognize your nature, you must receive the blessings of a guru who has the lineage. This transmission depends upon the disciple's devotion. It is not given just because you have a close relationship. It is therefore vital never to separate yourself from the devotion of seeing your guru as the dharmakaya buddha.

To that end, it will also be beneficial to persevere in the various ways of gathering the accumulations and purifying your obscurations. Without assembling any of these favorable causes and conditions, to just busy yourself with so much study and talk will help nothing. There are many who, in the time of real need, discover that they had been fooling themselves all along.

When, on the contrary, you gather within yourself the many causes, such as trust and devotion, you find that the compassionate influence of the gurus of the three times is beyond increase and decrease, and that you bathe in the blessings of the three roots. When that is the case, whatever you wish for among supreme and common attainments will come to you spontaneously. In this way, you will be a hero who accomplishes the welfare of both yourself and others. But looking at our present thoughts and deeds, this will hardly be more than wishful thinking. Nevertheless, if you are able to persevere, it will surely come to be. This is proven by the true statements of the vajra-holding conqueror and the authentic life examples of former masters. So keep this advice in your heart.

Even if I had expressed this advice in verse, the vital meaning would be no different. So to simplify the meaning, I expressed it here in prose. Through this goodness, may your mind be successful on the true path.

May it be helpful. May it be helpful. May it be helpful.

This was uttered by Padma Vijaya.[18]

Moreover, everything belonging to the world and beings, samsara and nirvana, is all the play, dance, and adornment of self-knowing awakened mind and is experienced as nothing other than that. This is like failing to find a single ordinary stone or clod of dirt when you have arrived on an island of pure gold. Likewise, as everything is utterly subsumed within the expanse of the single sphere, it is the originally free dzogchen beyond constructs. You can find this clearly explained in the

---

18. Padma Vijaya is a pen name of Shechen Gyaltsab. It appears that this line is here because Shechen Gyaltsab added the following addendum at a later date.

writings of Flawless Light Ray, who is Samantabhadra in person, as well in the writings of his lineage heirs.[19]

This fact was not created by wise buddhas nor forged by clever sentient beings. It cannot be bound through the golden concepts of clinging to a view and meditation, nor can it be polluted by the evil concepts that hold dualistic emotions. Right now, the true nature that has been present since the beginning—an original, coemergent wakefulness, the composure of intrinsic knowing—is simply the nature of mind in all of us: naked empty knowing.

This uncontrived natural state of ordinary mind is not a new invention formed by learned masters, nor is it newly produced through the disciple's excellent practice. But rather, it is an indelible and primordial presence within everyone's mindstream—from Samantabhadra down to and including the tiniest insect. Sentient beings, however, fail to acknowledge this, their own nature, like the metaphor of the lost prince who is forgotten among common people. Therefore, resolve that your uncontrived, fresh wakefulness is itself the dharmakaya mind of Samantabhadra.

Whatever experience unfolds, do not pollute it with the judgments of what should be kept or discarded, accepted or rejected. Rather, set free your undirected wakefulness in the unbridled vastness of free presence, and settle definitively on vast pervasiveness, free and unbound. Apart from that, it is essential not to spoil it with various attempts at modification and improvement, such as expecting something better, fear-

---

19. This refers to Longchenpa.

ing it will get worse, focusing elsewhere, concentrating on something as being here, encouraging stillness, discouraging thought movement, keeping a tally of arising and ceasing, making a split between lucid and empty, or any other value judgment about your experience.

In short, when your present wakefulness, fresh and naked, opens up as the heart of your training, you can be fully content with just that, without having to "change its coat or smooth its edges." Like the saying, "As water clears when undisturbed, the mind will clear when left uncontrived," it is also vital to settle in naturalness without polluting yourself with value judgments.

No matter how excellent you believe your assumptions, contrived view, and meditation states to be, they are nothing but different forms of clinging. As long as this clinging persists, you are still sowing the seeds for further samsara, just like Saraha sang:

Whatever you may cling to, let it go.
When this insight is yours, then everything is this.
No one will find an insight superior to this.

He also sang:

A sore from just a single husk
Can soon bring forth tremendous pain.

So it is of utmost importance to let your mind remain uncontrived.

As various thought forms—whether wholesome or unwholesome—unfold as the display of this mind, allow them just to be, uncontrived. Do not attempt to reject or accept, approve or disprove. By letting be in this way, everything will assist you in letting pristine wakefulness dawn. For this to dawn, you must receive the realized state of wakefulness of the ultimate transmission, for which you must receive the blessings of a guru. The receiving of such blessings depends entirely upon the disciple's trust and devotion, so keep this advice in mind.

This was spoken by the old Vijaya.

KEY POINTS
IN DZOGCHEN PRACTICE

A Carefree Vagrant
Shechen Gyaltsab, Pema Namgyal

Homage to the second buddha, Samyepa Kunkhyen Ngagi Wangpo.[20]

Here I shall briefly explain the key points of practice according to dzogchen.

First of all, on a comfortable seat assume the sevenfold posture of Vairochana in a relaxed and comfortable manner. Since the eyes are the gates for the manifestation of wisdom, in particular look straight ahead into the sky with wide-open eyes and without a focal support. As for the key point of speech, let your breathing flow naturally, not through your nose but very gently through your mouth. There is a reason for each of these points, so do not disregard them or think them unimportant.

---

20. Samyepa Kunkhyen Ngagi Wangpo refers to Longchenpa. He was known as Samyepa because he lived at Samye in Central Tibet for many years. Kunkhyen means the 'omniscient one,' and Ngagi Wangpo was one of his general names.

Following this, cultivate renunciation, weariness, compassion, and bodhichitta. After that, visualize your root guru above the crown of your head in his ordinary form, dress, and attire. Supplicate him, not just in mere words or platitudes, but with tear-filled devotion, so that realization of the profound path may quickly dawn within you. For the realization of dzogchen to occur in your mind, you must receive the transmission of the blessings from the mind of a master who possesses the lineage. This transmission depends upon the disciple's devotion, so it is of utmost importance. Without getting involved in too much chanting or forced practice, supplicate him one-pointedly. That is essential.

After this, according to the key points of visualization for receiving the four empowerments, mingle the guru's mind with your mind and sustain the innate essence of great bliss, which is empty cognizance free from fixation.

Here, meditation doesn't mean the cultivation of the absentminded, vacant, and indifferent state of the all-ground. Nor does it mean the cultivation of the conscious and tranquil state of the all-ground consciousness. Similarly, meditation doesn't mean to cultivate the blank state of a nonconceptual experience or the variegated thoughts that appear as objects.

Well, what is meditation then? When your past thought has ceased and your future thought has not yet arisen and you are free from conceptual reckoning in the present moment, then your genuine and natural awareness, the union of being empty and cognizant, dawns as the state of mind, which is like space—that itself is dzogchen transcending concepts, the cutting through of primordial purity, the open and naked exhaustion of phenomena.

This is exactly what you should recognize. To sustain the practice means simply to rest in naturalness after recognizing. In any context, whether it be view, meditation, or conduct, this is exactly what should be revealed in its naked state. Unless you experience and understand that, one teaching will tell you to be free from arising, dwelling, and ceasing, while another will claim, "It is such and such!" With these ideas in mind, you are simply naming the nameless. Within that mire of intellectual assumptions, you'll never find the chance for realization.

Dharmakaya is naked and empty awareness that transcends concepts and cannot, apart from a mere mental image, be established as having concrete existence by means of descriptive words or by the analytical intellect. But, when the blessings of your master coincide with the power of your own meditation practice, you will cut through misconceptions, just like a small child awakening to the faculty of intelligence. When this has happened, it is essential not to abandon your discovery but to cultivate it continuously with diligence.

While a beginner, if you get too slack, there is the risk of slipping into nonstop delusion, so you have to be constantly mindful.

Whether there is stillness, thought occurrence, or the noticing of them, it is essential to practice while looking directly into the fresh awareness of the observer.[21]

---

21. This sentence plays on the word *rig,* which appears in "observer" (*rig mkhan*), "noticing" (*rig*), and "awareness" (*rig pa*).

While meditating in this way, the sign of manifest awareness is when it seems that you have even more thought activity, agitation, and disturbing emotions than before. Also, an endless number of variations on the three experiences of bliss, clarity, and nonthought appear. But don't have hope or fear about them. Don't try to accept or reject them, or cling to or fixate on them in any way. Rather, practice while looking directly into the awareness that experiences them. In this way they become your friends. If you cling to or fixate on those experiences, you will simply get entangled in fixation.

If your mind gets drowsy or dull and the clarity of awareness is not manifest, you can clear such a state by visualizing the letter AH or a sphere of light in your heart center and projecting it out through the crown of your head. Pausing after your exhalation, imagine that the AH or sphere hovers in the air about the length of an arrow above you.

If you get too agitated, you can steady yourself by deeply relaxing your body and mind, lowering your gaze, and imagining a tiny sphere at the tip of your nose.

Sometimes, when there is a clear, cloudless sky, you can sit with your back to the sun, direct your eyes to the center of space, and breathe very gently, pausing briefly after each exhalation. By doing so, in an instant, the open and naked dharmakaya of awareness and emptiness will appear from within you. This realization of the threefold sky is a most profound instruction.

At others times, you can keep your body in the sevenfold posture, breathe naturally, and keep your mind free from thought. Then lie down on your back, stretch out your arms and legs, and let your eyes look into the sky. Forcefully exclaim HA! three times, sending your breath out. Then leave your mind in its natural state. By doing this, a realization of nonconceptual dharmata will take place.

Furthermore, when you rest in naturalness with your body in the sevenfold posture, don't dwell on whatever is perceived, but rest in the empty quality while focusing your gaze freely and easily in total openness, transcending outside, inside, and in-between. By doing this, a realization of space like emptiness will occur.

Again, don't dwell on the empty quality but rest in the nongrasping state of self-cognizant perception. By doing this, a realization of utterly insubstantial and unfixated perception will occur.

Once again, direct your attention to the thought activity arising from the clarity of awareness and you will have the realization that it is like a wave dissolving in water, liberated with neither support nor fixation.

These instructions are profound methods that result in direct personal experience. In this way, you give rise to certainty within yourself.

In short, the meditation of innate awareness that I mentioned before—the realization of primordial purity in which phenomena are exhausted; the transcendence of good and evil, faults and virtues; the absence of attaining and clearing away, change and alteration; the wisdom beyond dualistic concepts; the final point of realization, whether it be madhyamaka, mahamudra, or dzogchen—is itself present at all times, and that is exactly what you should recognize.

While doing so, don't concentrate with deliberate effort and don't get dissipated through distraction. Sustain the yoga of unfabricated naturalness like the steady flow of a river. This is the essence of practice.

Whatever takes place at this point, whether it be the six types of cognition, thoughts relating to the five poisons, or fluctuations in temporary experiences, all manifests as a display of the expression of awareness, bodhichitta. They are equal in appearing, they are equally empty, they are equally real and also equally false. All of them are nothing but the magical display of awareness, so don't get involved in negating or approving, accepting or rejecting, clinging to or fixating on them as something to be discarded or as a remedy. Rather, relax openly and free from fixation into the fresh state of awareness of that which experiences. In this way it is essential to train the strength of your realization by naturally liberating whatever arises.

Here, the term shamatha is given to the aspect of stillness, and vipashyana to the aspect of directly realizing wide-open awareness and emptiness. They have different names but in fact are indivisible.

By realizing that the essence of awareness is empty, you are free from the extreme of eternalism, and by seeing that the nature is cognizant, you are liberated from the extreme of nihilism. By avoiding the hope of cultivating the experiences of bliss, clarity, and nonthought, you are liberated from the states of the three realms. By destroying the fixation of remedy, no defilement or error will remain in your nature.

Don't expect to attain enlightenment in the future within

the mire of mind-made assumptions; instead take as your path the three kayas that are naturally present within you at this very moment. That itself is the special quality of dzogchen. For the practitioner who realizes this, the sun of happiness will shine from within, no matter where he or she resides.

Obstacles and sidetracks all result from hope and fear, and from clinging to and fixating on things as real. Therefore, it is essential to avoid fixating on anything whatsoever.

Whatever you experience, whether it be sickness in your body, pain in your mind, a "real" disturbing emotion, clinging and fixation, accepting or rejecting, identify it and supplicate your master and receive his blessings. Minutely examine and track down—not just as a rough understanding—the mind that accepts or rejects. From where did it arise, where does it remain, and to where does it go?

By doing this you will find that it doesn't exist as anything whatsoever and it doesn't remain anywhere either. Thus, you cannot possibly avoid experiencing a wakefulness that transcends the notions of perceiver and perceived and cannot be described in words. That is dharmakaya—naked and aware emptiness. When this experience takes place, sustain the state of exactly that and all your obstacles and sidetracks will be naturally liberated.

Devotion to the master is the king of all enhancement practices, so give up regarding him as an ordinary human being. It is essential never to separate yourself from the devotion of seeing him as a buddha in person.

Moreover, if you alternate between meditation on impermanence, compassion, development stage, and completion stage with and without attributes, each practice will enhance the other. This will be most effective.

At the end of your sessions, never forget to make dedication.

In the breaks never forget the practice of regarding all phenomena as magical apparitions.

At night, practice the yoga of sleep. When about to fall asleep, supplicate so that you can experience the sleeping state as luminosity. After that, mingle the master with your mind, sustaining the fresh state of awareness. While doing so, go to sleep without being interrupted by any other thoughts.

There are further points to understand. Unless you resolve the view, you won't be able to destroy the bonds that cling to the notion of a perceiver and a perceived, thinking them to be real. During the meditation state, it is essential to resolve that all phenomena are nonexistent, pervasive, spontaneously present, and oneness.[22]

Unless you sustain continuity in meditation, you won't arrive at the vital point. Simply assuming that the view is such and such is not enough. It is essential to maintain meditation constantly with diligence.

Unless you differentiate between good and bad conduct, there is the risk that you will stray into total negativity, thinking that both good and evil are empty. The key point is to change whatever you do during post-meditation into a virtuous action by maintaining the feeling that everything is like a magical apparition and having firm confidence in the belief that the law of karma is infallible.

---

22. These are the famous four samayas of *Dzogchen* practice.

If you separate means and knowledge, you will always remain in bondage. It is essential to embark on the highway that delights the victorious ones: the unity of emptiness and compassion and of the two accumulations of merit and wisdom.

These are extremely important key points, so keep them in mind in this way:

> Unless the feeling of impermanence and weariness
>   arises in my mind,
> The business of appearing to practice in this life
> Will never provide a chance to genuinely accomplish the
>   sacred Dharma.
> May real renunciation dawn within me.
> Unless I train in compassion and the excellent
>   bodhichitta,
> In the darkness of clinging to selfish aims,
> There will never be a chance to illuminate the excellent
>   path of Mahayana.
> May I train in true and eminent bodhichitta.
> I commit acts that seem to benefit others,
> Although I have not reached the state of a noble being.
> These acts, in fact, don't help others and cause me to
>   fetter myself.
> Without fooling myself with distractions and bustle,
> May I practice diligently in secluded places.
> Means and knowledge separated are like a man with a
>   broken leg,

Who lacks the power to journey the paths and bhumis
  to omniscience.
While uniting emptiness and compassion, development
  and completion, and the two accumulations,
May I embark on the unmistaken path.
Without receiving the blessings of a master endowed
  with the lineage,
I won't realize the natural state by endeavoring in my
  practice.
Through an auspicious coincidence of perfect devotion,
May I obtain the supreme empowerment transmitting
  the lineage of realization.
Dzogchen beyond concepts, luminous self-awareness,
Is the spontaneous presence of kayas and wisdoms from
  the beginning.
Through the instruction of freely resting in the innate
  mode,
May I attain stability in the level of exhaustion.
When the time arrives to bring benefit to beings,
May I don the armor of never tiring to help others.
May I alone liberate my infinite mothers
From the river of samsaric existence.

This upadesha *for the benefit of beginners was given to a friend with the
name Kamali, by the yogi Yanpa Lodey (Carefree Vagrant).*[23]

Completed for the time being! ITHI!

---

23. Carefree Vagrant was another of Shechen Gyaltsab's pen names.

Unity

NATURALLY LIBERATING WHATEVER YOU MEET

Instructions to Guide You on the Profound Path

Khenpo Gangshar

With the devotion of self-cognizance, I pay homage to Guru Vajradhara.

A worthy student is one who aspires to practice the profoundest of the profound and secret Vajrayana—the essential oral instructions of all the *anuttarayoga* tantras or the nature of the realization of effortless *ati*. To meet the needs of such a student, the following three points should be taught:

1. The preliminary steps of mind training.
2. The main part of the practice.
3. The subsequent application, combining the profound advice into key points.

THE PRELIMINARIES

The first of these is in two parts: the general preliminaries and the special preliminaries, which represent the unique qualities of this particular path.

The General Preliminaries

First of all, you should practice the following steps according to the general teachings:

Taking refuge, which is the difference between this path and an incorrect path.

Arousing bodhichitta, which raises you above the inferior paths.

Performing the meditation and recitation of Vajrasattva, which purifies the misdeeds, obscurations, and adverse conditions that prevent the essence of refuge and bodhichitta from dawning in your being.

Offering the mandala, which is the method for gathering the accumulations, the harmonious conditions.

Performing the guru yoga, the root of blessings and the means by which the special qualities of experience and realization quickly arise in your being.

The Special Preliminaries

Next are the special preliminaries that, according to this system of teachings, are called the analytic meditation of a pandita.

It is an unfailing fact that happiness results from virtuous action and that suffering results from having committed unvirtuous karmic deeds. Therefore, you must first recognize what is virtuous and what is evil. In order to do this, you must determine which is most important: your body, speech, or mind. In order to decide this, you must understand what your body, speech, and mind are.

Your body is your physical body that serves as the support for benefit and harm. Your speech is the making of sounds and talking. Your mind is that which can think of and recollect anything at all—that which feels like or dislike and shows different expressions of joy and sorrow from one moment to the next. This briefly explains the body, speech, and mind.

When you commit a virtuous or unvirtuous action, you must ask yourself, "Is the body the main thing? Is the speech the primary aspect? Or is the mind most important?" Some people will reply that it is the body, some that it is the speech, and some will say that the mind is the primary aspect. In any case, whoever claims that the body or speech is most important has not really penetrated to the core with their examination.

It is the mind that is the most important. The reason is that unless your mind intends to do so, your body cannot possibly do anything good or bad. Nor can your voice express anything good or evil. Your mind is therefore the primary factor. As it is said,

The mind rules over everything like a king;
The body is a servant for all good or evil deeds.

In that way, your mind is like a king, and both your body and speech are its servants.

For instance, when you get angry with an enemy, you must examine whether the primary factor is your mind or the enemy. Similarly, when you feel attached to a friend, examine whether your mind or the friend is the primary factor. Examining in this way, you must acknowledge that although the friend and enemy are the circumstances in which attachment and anger arise, the real cause originates in your own mind. Thus, your mind is most important.

Once you master your own mind, neither friend nor enemy will be able to benefit or harm you. If you don't gain control over your mind, then, wherever you go and wherever you stay, attachment and anger will automatically well up. You must understand that your mind is the root of all joy and sorrow, good and evil, attachment and anger. The Great Omniscient One, Longchenpa, has said,

> When under the influence of datura,
> All the various experiences you have, whatever they may be,
> Are all, in fact, mistaken images without existence.
> Likewise, understand that under the influence of a confused
>   mind,
> All the mistaken experiences of the six classes of beings,
>   whatever they might be,
> Are all empty images, nonexistent yet appearing.
> Since they appear in your mind and are constructed by your
>   mind,
> Exert yourself in taming this mistaken mind.

That is how it is. But you shouldn't take your understanding from books or stories heard from others. Instead, recognize for yourself that appearance is mind and understand that your mind is the root of all phenomena.

In this context, you must distinguish between appearance (*nangwa*) and the perceived object (*nang-yul*).[24] Without doing that, it will be like the Great Omniscient One stated:

Ignorant people claim that everything is mind.
They are deluded about the three types of appearance,
Have many shortcomings, mix things up, and over
exaggerate.
Meditators, give up such unwholesome ways!

A perceived object is the mere presence of a visible form, sound, or the like, that is an object of any of the six types of consciousness. Thoughts of attachment, anger, or delusion based on the perceived objects are appearances, for example, the feeling of attachment to a pleasant object, the feeling of anger towards an unpleasant one, and the indifferent feeling towards something neutral. You must understand that such appearances are the functions of your own mind.

Due to mind, perceived objects such as form, sound, and so forth, have appeared, but they are not mind—they are the

---

24. Tulku Urgyen Rinpoche explains these two terms in the following way: The perceived object is not mind; it is under the power of mind. Without a condition, the perceived object will not appear. All appearances, outer, inner, and of the bardo, no matter how subtle, emerge with no true existence, due to confused mind. In dzogchen, there is the original misapprehension of the five colored lights seen as the five objects. They are an expression of mind, under the power of mind, but not mind.

shared appearances of sentient beings and do not possess any true existence, besides being phenomena of dependent origination.

You should now examine where this mind dwells: from the top of the hair on your head to the nails on your toes; from the outer layer of skin, the flesh in between, to the bones, five organs, and six vessels within. When investigating the dwelling place of mind, most Chinese will claim that it abides in the head. Tibetans will say that it dwells in the heart. Neither one is sure, because when you touch the top of the head, the mind seems to leap there, and when you touch the soles of the feet, it seems to jump there. It has no fixed place. It dwells neither in outer objects, nor inside the body, nor in the empty space in between. You must become certain that it has no dwelling place.

If your mind has a dwelling place, what are the outer, inner, and middle aspects of this dwelling place? Is it identical with or different from the dweller? If they are identical—since there is increase or decrease, change and alteration, in outer objects and within the body—your mind will change in the very same way. So it is illogical to think they are identical.

If they are different, then is the essence of this different mind something that exists or not? If it is, then it should at least have a shape and color. Since there is no shape or color, it does not unilaterally exist. However, since this ever-conscious and ever-aware king is unceasing, it does not unilaterally not exist.

For this reason the glorious Karmapa Rangjung Dorje proclaimed:

It is not existent since even the victorious ones do not see it.
It is not nonexistent since it is the basis of samsara and
*   nirvana.*
This is not a contradiction, but the middle way of unity.
May we realize the nature of mind, free from extremes.[25]

The explanation up to this point completes the preliminary teachings of the analytical meditation of a pandita.

THE MAIN PART OF PRACTICE

The second part, the steps of the teachings on the main part of the practice, the resting meditation of a kusulu, is presented under two points:

1. Pointing out the nature of body, speech, and mind by means of the instruction in resolving.
2. Pointing out dualistic mind and awareness, one by one, by means of the instruction in distinguishing.

Resolving

Keep your body straight, refrain from talking, open your mouth slightly, and let the breath flow naturally. Don't pursue the past and don't invite the future. Simply rest naturally in the naked ordinary mind of the immediate present without trying to correct it or replace it. If you rest like that, your mind-essence will be clear and expansive, vivid and naked,

---

25. This verse is found in *The Mahamudra Aspiration of True Meaning*.

without any concerns about thought or recollection, joy or pain. That is awareness (*rigpa*).

At the same time, there is no thought such as, "Sights and sounds are out there!" Unobstructed, everything appears. There is also no thought such as, "The perceiver, the six types of consciousness, is within!" Clear and nonconceptual, naked awareness is unceasing.

While in that state, your body is left to itself without fabrication, free and easy. That is the body of all the victorious ones. That is the essence of the development stage.

Your speech is free from fabrication, without efforts to track down the root of sound, but simply expressing directly and openly whatever comes to mind. It is all-pervasive from the very moment that it is heard, a nonarising, empty resounding. That is the speech of all the victorious ones. It is the essence of all recitation.

When you rest your mind in unfabricated naturalness, no matter what thought may arise, good or bad, happy or sad, the mind-essence that is free from concerns about joy or sorrow is clear and empty, naked and awake. This mind-essence is the nature of all sentient beings, the realization of the buddhas of the three times, the essence of the eighty-four thousand Dharma doors, and the heart of the glorious master, the supreme guide. It is the transcendent knowledge of the second set of teachings and the sugata essence of the last turning of the wheel of the Dharma. According to the general system of mantra, it is called continuity of ground, the spontaneously present mandala of the innate nature. According to the anuttarayoga tantras, it is called Guhyasamaja, Chakrasamvara, Kalachakra, and so forth. As for the three inner tantras, according to *mahayoga*, it is the great dharmakaya of the exalted inseparability of the two truths; according to *anuyoga*, it is the basic mandala of bodhichitta of the child known as great bliss; according to *atiyoga*, it is dzogchen of awareness and emptiness.

All these renowned expressions point a finger at this mind-essence itself, and nothing else. This point is also presented in the Gelug school, as stated by the great lord Tsongkhapa:

> *Appearance, the unfailing dependent origination,*
> *And emptiness, understanding beyond statements—*
> *As long as these two seem to be separate,*
> *You have still not realized the intent of Shakyamuni.*
> *When all at once and without fluctuation*
> *Your conviction and your notion of an object fall apart,*
> *That is the moment of having completed the analysis of*
> *   the view.*

The lord of Dharma, Drakpa Gyaltsen, has said, "When you have clinging, it is not the view." The Dharma masters of the Sakya School regard their view of undivided samsara and nirvana to be nonfixation. Moreover, according to the matchless Kagyüpa masters, the glorious Karmapa Rangjung Dorje proclaimed:

> *Nothing is true or false,*
> *Like moons in water, say the wise.*
> *This ordinary mind itself is the dharma expanse, the essence*
> *   of the victors,*
> *Thus, the luminous mahamudra is also nonfixation.*

It is said that all the learned and accomplished masters of India and Tibet had the same realization, and there is not a single master who claims that the realization of the main part of practice is anything other than nonfixation. That is the meaning you yourself should understand and point out to others.

This completes the section that indicates that your body, speech, and mind are the enlightened body, speech, and mind of the victorious ones. It has the same meaning as in the verses by the great master of Uddiyana, that begin with, "Do this towards all that you see," and so forth.[26]

Distinguishing

It is very important to distinguish the difference between mind (*sem*) and awareness (*rigpa*). The Great Omniscient One said:

> *The big oxen pretending to know ati these days*
> *Claim that discursive thinking is awakened mind.*
> *Such ignorant people, in their realm of darkness,*
> *Are far away from the meaning of dzogchen.*

If you fail to distinguish between mind and awareness, you will likely engage in conduct that confuses cause and result, and thus turn away from the path in which view and conduct are united.

When experiencing the continuity of undistracted naturalness, awareness is free from a reference point, like space; and it has not even a speck of joy or sorrow, hope or fear,

---

26. This is a well-known quote from the "Supplication in Seven Chapters."

PERFECT CLARITY

benefit or harm, whether you meet with positive or negative conditions.

The character of mind is evident the moment you get slightly distracted and encounter conditions that give rise to your feeling joy or sorrow. Having given rise to joy or sorrow, you will accumulate karmic actions.

For example, mind is like the clouds gathering in the sky. Therefore, you must gain stability in awareness (*rigpa*), which is like a cloudless sky. You must be able to purify the aspect of mind that is like the clouds in the sky. Through this you will be able to separate mind and awareness.

THE PROFOUND ADVICE

The third part explains the profound advice on the subsequent application based on the oral instructions that reveal direct self-liberation.

While you remain in undistracted naturalness, it is utterly impossible to accumulate karma, and you have cut the stream of further accumulation of karma. While not accumulating new karma, do not get the idea that there is neither good nor evil to be experienced, for past karma still ripens. That is, unless you purify all the karmic deeds you have previously accumulated through confession, purification, and so forth, they will ripen without fail. The ripening of karma is still possible.

This ripening will manifest in your body or mind and nowhere else. When it ripens in your body, you will fall sick. When it ripens in your mind, you will feel joy or sorrow and the thoughts of the six types of disturbing emotions will arise. When this happens, it is important to possess the oral instructions on taking sickness as the path, taking joy and sorrow as the path, taking disturbing emotions as the path, and so forth. But simply resting in naturalness, the essence of all these applications is sufficient unto itself.

If you feel happy when meeting with good conditions and sad when encountering negative circumstances, and if you indulge in the feeling of happiness when happy and the feeling of sadness when sad, then you will accumulate immense karma. Therefore, you must immediately recognize a thought, be it happy or sad, in any circumstance, positive or negative.

After recognition, you should rest in naturalness. Look into the one who feels happy or sad, without repressing one feeling or encouraging the other. Your clear, empty, and naked mind-essence, free from any concern about joy or sorrow, freely becomes the innate state of awareness.

Furthermore, when your body falls sick, don't indulge in the illness, but rest in naturalness. Look into the painful sensation itself. The pain doesn't cease when resting like that, however you will directly realize the innate state of awareness free from any thought about where it hurts, what hurts, how it hurts, as well as the subject and object of the pain. At that moment the sickness grows less intense and becomes somewhat insubstantial.

A person who has one disturbing emotion will possess the others as well. But due to the differences in people, some will have more anger, some more stinginess, some more dullness, some more desire, some more envy, and some will have a greater portion of pride. That is why there are different buddha families:

> The disturbing emotion of anger is an agitated state of mind caused by a painful sensation based on an unpleasant object.

> Stinginess is the inability to give away to others some attractive object because of retaining a tight clinging to possessing it.

> Dullness is like darkness. It is the root of all evil, for it is the lack of recognizing one's essence, and hence it obscures the true nature of things.

> Desire is to accept, long for, and feel attached to pleasant things, like sights or sounds, and so forth. In particular, carnal lust for the union of male and female is the primary attachment.

> Envy is to reject, and therefore disapprove of, the virtues of someone who is higher or equal to oneself.

> Pride is to regard others as lower and to feel superior in either religious or mundane matters.

These six disturbing emotions create the causes for the existence of the six classes of beings, such as rebirth in the hells through a predominance of anger.

Whenever one of these six arises, you must recognize it immediately. When recognizing it, don't reject it, don't accept it, just rest in naturalness, looking into that particular disturbing emotion. At that same moment, it is self-liberated and is called mirror-like wisdom, and so on. This is mentioned in a song from the *Second Treasury* of Ratna Lingpa:

> *The essence of your angry mind is clear awareness,*
> *Bright and empty the moment you recognize it.*
> *This nature is called mirror-like wisdom.*
> *Young maid, let's rest in the natural state.*

> *The essence of your dull mind is clear self-awareness,*
> *Wide-awake the moment you look into your natural face.*
> *This vital nature is called dharmadhatu wisdom.*
> *Young maid, let's rest in the natural state.*

> *The essence of your proud mind is the unfolding of self-*
> *awareness,*
> *Naturally empty the moment you rest, looking into your*
> *natural face.*
> *This state is called the wisdom of equality.*
> *Young maid, let's rest in the natural state.*

> *The essence of your lustful mind is, no doubt, attachment,*
> *The state of empty bliss, the moment you sustain it without*
> *clinging.*
> *This nature is called discriminating wisdom.*
> *Young maid, let's rest in the natural state.*

That is how it is.

However, if you regard disturbing emotions as faults and reject them, they may be temporarily suppressed but not cut from their root. Consequently, at some point, the poisonous remnant will reemerge, as is the case of the mundane *dhyana* states. On the one hand, when you regard disturbing emotions as emptiness, your practice turns into "taking emptiness as the path" rather than the disturbing emotions. Thus your practice doesn't become the short path, the special quality of mantra. On the other hand, if you indulge in the disturbing emotions, thinking they are something concrete, it is like eating a poisonous plant and is the cause that binds you to samsara, just like the copulation of ordinary people.

For these reasons, just as poison can be extracted from a poisonous plant and taken as a medicine, the special quality of this teaching lies in the fact that any disturbing emotion that may arise is wisdom the moment you relax in naturalness. Look directly into it—don't deliberately reject it, regard it as a fault, indulge in it concretely, or regard it as a virtue.

Beyond this, if you are interested in the system of direct instructions, such as the teachings on the path of means, you must learn them in detail from the oral instructions of your master.

Taking the Bardo as the Path

When you press your fingers on your ears or on your eyes, sounds naturally resound or colors and lights naturally manifest. Rest naturally for a long time and grow accustomed to the appearance of utterly empty forms that don't exist anywhere—neither outside, inside, nor in between. Since, at the time of death, there is nothing other than this, you will recognize these sounds, colors, and lights as your own self-display and be liberated, just like meeting a person you already know, or like a child leaping onto its mother's lap.

This teaching corresponds to the key point of darkness instruction among the daylight and darkness instructions for practicing the manifest aspect of the *togal* of spontaneous presence. There are also the systems of practice based on the rising and setting rays of the sun during the day and on moonlight, electric light, and lamps at night.

Taking Sleep as the Path

Without depending on mental effort, such as emanations or transformations during the dream state, sleep in a state of undistracted naturalness. During that time, you may slip into deep sleep devoid of dreams. As soon as you awake, you are vividly clear in the natural state. This is called the luminosity of deep sleep.

It may happen that sleep doesn't occur at all, but instead, you remain awake and vividly clear. Or you fall asleep, yet though various dreams take place, they are forgotten the moment you wake up the next morning with nothing to remember. That is the beginning of having purified dreams. For the person of the highest capacity and diligence, it is said that dreams cease by being forgotten. For the intermediate person they cease by being recognized. For the person of lesser capacity they cease through the experience of excellent dreams.

The fact that dreaming must eventually be purified is commonly agreed upon in all the sutras, tantras, and treatises.

The additional points about the practice of *phowa* should be learned from other sources. These teachings were merely a condensation of the basic points of the instructions.

> From the core of realization of all the victorious ones
>   and their sons,
> The root advice of the profound points of the new and
>   old tantras,
> I have extracted the fresh essence of the profound oral
>   instructions
> And written them down concisely.
> It is taught that in these times, when it is difficult to
>   tame beings through the vehicles of effort,
> The teachings of effortless mind will appear.
> By the power of the times,[27] if you practice these points,
> They are a teaching that is easy to apply and devoid of
>   error.
> At a time when I saw many reasons
> And was requested to do so by several eminent people,
> Setting aside elaborate poetry and lengthy expressions,
> This was written by Gangshar Wangpo, a khenpo from
>   Shechen,
> Naturally and freely, in a way that is pleasant to hear
>   and easy to understand.

---

27. "The times" refers to the Chinese invasion of Tibet in the 1950s; these teachings were specifically given to deal with the forthcoming difficulties.

By this virtue, may an infinite number of beings
Be victorious in the battle with the demigods of
    platitude,
May they shine with the majestic brilliance of the
    essence of profound meaning,
And may there be a celebration of a new golden age.

Sarva dakalayanam bhavantu.

Tsele Natsok Rangdrol

COGNIZANCE

The Instruction that Points Out
the Basis of Flawless Meditation

Tsele Natsok Rangdrol

The eminent vidyadhara Menpa Gomchen has told me that I must clarify the actual meaning of the word "cognizance" (*salwa*) as it has been used in my writings so far. So I will now explain what it means.

At the beginning, the cause and condition for confusion to arise for all sentient beings, and for their wandering in samsara, lies in failing to recognize that the experience (*nangwa*) of the cognizant quality manifesting from the all-ground is a natural display (*rangdang*) and, instead, believing it to be separate objects. I have explained how one is then deluded by fixating on self and other as being separate, and so on, at the start of my notes on mahamudra and dzogchen.[28]

_____

28. Tsele Natsok Rangdrol is the author of *The Mirror of Mindfulness, The Lamp of Mahamudra,* and *Circle of the Sun.*

Now, while practicing the path, all the outer and inner perceptions arise from this quality of unceasing cognizance, the natural display of the intangible empty essence of mind. In other words, all the objects of the six senses—the outer visible forms, sounds, scents, aromas, and textures—are this cognizant quality without a single exception. The inner visual, auditory, olfactory, gustatory, physical, and mental sensations, and their corresponding attractions and aversions, are also this cognizance, without any exception. Thus all outer and inner things, without a single omission, are exclusively the manifestations of the cognizant quality of one's own mind. That is called cognizance.

Believing that, if there were no cognizant quality, there would be no delusion, no wandering in samsara, no practice to apply, no practitioner, and no result of the practice, which unavoidably leads to falling into the extreme of the blank void of nihilism. It is for this reason that how to apply this cognizant quality in one's experience is explained in all the practices of the higher and lower vehicles, and particularly in the context of meditation practice.

Furthermore, some meditators these days, having not been accepted by a qualified master and thus never having received genuine instructions, believe that the manifestation of the cognizant quality of their mind is not meditation practice and try forcibly to suppress it. Thus there are many people who assume that meditation is nothing other than a nonconceptual state. Having made such an assumption, their meditation turns into a shamatha stupor and never becomes mahamudra or dzogchen. This is definitely not the path of enlightenment.

In the end, upon realizing the fruition, it becomes apparent that all the qualities of knowledge, loving kindness, enlightened deeds, compassion, and so forth, are the power and effect of this cognizance as well. So if cognizance is inhibited now at the time of the path, how can the knowledge and compassion, and so on, manifest later at the time of fruition? Consequently, these are the reasons why taking cognizance as the path is the root of practice.

Now, how do we take cognizance as the path? No matter what thought you have or what perception occurs, don't grasp it as being solid and don't follow after it. Don't try to block it. And don't attempt to do anything else, such as using a remedy or a change of focus. Simply recognize natural awareness (*rangrig*), and let the thought or perception dissipate on its own. Leave it be; let it go where it wants.

When you don't stray from this fresh ordinary mind no matter what takes place, then simply to avoid fixating on good and bad, accepting and rejecting, is itself sufficient. That is the practice of self-cognizant natural awareness. In short, your present thought or thinking is itself this cognizance. That within you that merely knows, recollects, or notices is called mindfulness, self-awareness, contemplation, or insight. All the different Dharma systems agree that it is sufficient to practice just like this as the meditation.

No matter what kind of seemingly more superior meditation state you may achieve, such as stillness or bliss, clarity or nonthought, it is nothing but a fabrication. Consequently, it is not uncreated, unfabricated ordinary mind and hence not a flawless meditation. Therefore you must gain a positive certainty about this point. Please understand this.

VIEW AND MEDITATION

Jamgon Kongtrul

NAMO GURU

View and meditation can be explained in many ways,
But sustaining the essence of your mind includes
    them all.
Your mind won't be found elsewhere;
It is just your present thought.

Don't chase after that thought,
Just look into its essence.
There is no duality—no observer, nothing observed.

It is empty—not a concrete substance.
It is cognizant—aware by itself.
These two are not separate, but a unity.
Nothing whatsoever, yet everything is experienced.
Simply recognize this!

With constant mindfulness, sustain this recognition.
Cultivate nothing but this.
Let it remain naturally.
Don't spoil it by tampering and worrying about being
    right or wrong.
The ultimate luminosity of dharmakaya is this
    unfabricated, ordinary mind.

Though there are many Dharma words in mahamudra
    and dzogchen,
The root of practice is included herein.
If you search elsewhere for something better,
A "buddha" superior to this,
You are chained by hope and fear—so give it up!

Devotion and gathering the accumulations are the most
    important methods
For completely realizing this teaching.
Always concentrate on devotion
To the guru, the Lord of Uddiyana,
And apply your body, speech, and mind to what is
    virtuous.

MANGALAM.

LIBERATION THROUGH HEARING IN THE BARDO

Verses on the Bardo from the Six Wonderful
Methods for Enlightenment without Cultivation

Guru Rinpoche
Revealed by Chokgyur Lingpa

Here I shall explain the profound meaning of liberation
through hearing for the one who has reached the time of
death. Among the three kinds of bardos, the first is the bardo
of dying:

> *Fortunate one of noble family, listen one-pointedly with*
> *mindfulness and no distraction. Whatever appears in this*
> *world is the illusory deception of Mara. Everything im-*
> *permanent is subject to death. Noble one, abandon suf-*
> *fering!*
>   *The experiences of whiteness, redness, and black-*
> *ness are all the magical display of your mind. These ap-*

pearances are nothing other than you, yourself. Don't be
afraid or shocked.

Now it seems that you are losing consciousness. Outer
appearances resemble the sky at dawn. Inner experience
resembles a butter lamp in a vase. Remain one-pointedly
in the clarity of nonthought. This luminosity of death is
buddha-mind itself. Rest naturally without fabricating
or distorting anything. Noble one, in this way you will
be liberated into dharmakaya.

Give this advice in a pleasant and clear manner. Those
of the highest capacity will be liberated through this. Now
comes the second bardo of dharmata:

Fortunate one of noble family, listen with undistracted,
one-pointed mindfulness. Earlier, you did not recognize
awareness. For the next seven days, all experiences will
arise as rainbows, lights, rays, spheres, and as the bodies
of deities. All are the magical display of the means and
knowledge of the five buddhas. Do not be afraid or ter-
rified by the brilliant colors and lights. Resolve that they
are your own expressions.

Together with these lights, dull-colored lights will also
appear and attract your mind. Do not be attached to them.
They are the self-display of the five poisons, the pathways
of samsara. Your experience will arise as pure and impure
paths, so do not miss the right path to be chosen.

From the heart centers of the male and female bud-
dhas of the five families, shafts of light reach your eyes.

This is the great, direct path of Vajrasattva. Quietly abide in awareness and pray, "Look upon me with compassion!" Supplicate with intense yearning. Without accepting or rejecting, without sending away or holding on to anything, maintain the state in which the appearances of deities are inseparable from you. At that time, as one deity dissolves into another, you will be liberated into sambhogakaya.

Listen, fortunate one! If you are not liberated now, know that time does not change though phenomena do. Everywhere in the four cardinal and four intermediate directions, above and below, amidst a roaring mass of flames and rainbow colors, is the Great and Glorious Heruka. His assembly of deities and terrifying attendants rain down sharp weapons, HUNG, PHAT, and laughter. This fiery spectacle of immense variety makes the one billion world systems tremble.

Without being afraid or terrified, recognize everything as the display of your awareness. Be firm in this and rest while mingling inseparably with the natural state. Having entered the path, you will be liberated.

In this way, those of the middle capacity are liberated. Thirdly, during the bardo of becoming, say to the dead person:

Listen, child of noble family. Maintain mindfulness and do not be distracted. Your body is now comprised of prana and mind. Around it the appearances of the bardo of

*becoming arise. Knowing you are dead, you long to be
alive. You are caught by the fierce servants of the Lord
of the Dead. Frightening sounds and steep defiles appear
along with many definite and indefinite signs. All this
is the manifestation of your mind, which is ultimately
empty like the sky. Space cannot be harmed by space.
Therefore, develop unconditioned confidence.*

*This consecrated substance, burnt and offered, is
an inexhaustible feast, the food of undefiled liberation
through hearing. Partake of it, and without attachment
to being alive, turn with longing to your yidam and
master.*

*To the west of here is the Blissful Realm where Lord
Amitabha dwells. Whoever recalls his name will be born
there. You, too, while recalling his name, should make
prayers. Generate devotion, thinking, "Care for me,
Lokeshvara and Guru Rinpoche!" Free of doubt, move
with a spontaneous vajra leap. In that buddha field,
within the hollow of a lotus bud, you will be swiftly and
miraculously born. Therefore, noble one, with delight
and joy give rise to devotion.*

Those of the lowest capacity are liberated like this. If not,
now comes the way of liberation once one has passed through
to rebirth:

*Listen, child of noble family. Since you have not closed
the door to the womb, when you see a log, a hollow*

*space, a dark place, a forest, or a palace, abandon desire
and clinging.*

*Make up your mind to be born on the Earth and
specifically in Tibet[29] in the presence of your teacher.*

*Visualize your future parents, from a religious family, as Guru Rinpoche and his consort. Abandon desire or
anger, and with faith enter the state of composure. Having become a vessel for the profound Dharma, you will
swiftly attain wisdom.*

Through these gradual instructions, no matter how low
one's capacity may be, one will certainly be liberated within
seven rebirths.

Draw the session to a close with the dedication and aspiration prayers and rest in the natural state of the pure nature
of all phenomena. A deeply profound instruction such as this
does not require cultivation, but liberates through hearing.

This teaching was extracted from a text in volume 1 of
the Chokling Tersar, called *Sheldam Nyingjang, The Essence
Manual of Oral Instructions.*

---

29. Today the aspiration must direct one to at any place where the Vajrayana
teachings are available.

Guru Rinpoche

THE ULTIMATE CONFESSION
OF SIMPLICITY

Guru Rinpoche
Revealed by Chokgyur Lingpa

Ah
Dharmadhatu itself is devoid of fabrications.
How mistaken we are to regard it as dual, like good
and bad!
How deluded to attribute characteristics to things!
I confess this in the expanse of great bliss free from
fabrications.

Samantabhadra is devoid of being good and bad.
How tiring to regard him as dual, like good and bad!
How pitiful it is to hold him as pure or impure.
I confess this in the expanse free from good and bad.

Bodhichitta is devoid of birth and death.
How tiring to regard it as being now and later!

How deluded to hold it as being born or dying!
I confess this in the expanse of unchanging immortality.

The great sphere is devoid of sides and corners.
How tiring to regard it as having form and substance!
How deluded to hold it as the duality of sides and
    corners!
I confess this in the ever-circular great sphere.

The state is unchanging throughout the three times,
How tiring to regard it as having beginning and end!
How deluded to hold it as the duality of transformation
    and change!
I confess this in the unchanging great sphere.

The self-existing wisdom is not to be sought for.
How tiring to regard it as the duality of cause and effect!
How deluded to hold the duality of effort and
    attainment!
I confess this in the self-existing expanse of
    effortlessness.

Awareness wisdom is devoid of permanence and
    interruption.
How tiring to regard it as the duality of permanence
    and interruption!
How deluded to view it as existence or nonexistence!
I confess this in the wisdom space free from permanence
    and interruption.

The pure dharmadhatu is devoid of center and edge.
How tiring to project or dissolve partiality to center or
 edge!
How deluded to claim it has center or edge!
I confess this in the pure dharmadhatu free from center
 or edge.

The celestial palace is devoid of outside and inside.
How tiring to regard it as having outside and inside!
How deluded to hold it as the duality of being wide or
 narrow!
I confess this in the space free from being wide or
 narrow, outside or inside.

The space of the mother is devoid of high and low.
How tiring to regard it as the duality of above and
 below!
How deluded to hold the duality of high and low!
I confess this in the bhaga free from being wide and
 narrow.

Dharmakaya is devoid of divisions.
How tiring to regard it as objects and mind!
How deluded to hold the duality of world and beings!
I confess this in the space of nondual wisdom.

Whatever is done or experienced is nothing but the
 display of the father.
How tiring to regard it as individual thoughts!

How deluded to misapprehend it with names!
I confess this in the space free from fixating on the display.

Awareness wisdom has not arisen from within.
How sad is this ignorant and deluded mind!
It perceives the formless phenomena as concrete and
 having attributes.
I openly confess this in the natural space of wisdom.

When not realizing the nature of nonarising,
How miserable is the mind of the mistaken individual!
It apprehends the nonarising phenomena as ego and
 self.
I openly confess this in the nonarising space of great bliss.

When the nature of dharmata is not cognized in the
 mind,
One does not understand that appearance and existence
 are illusory
And so gives rise to attachment to material things and
 wealth.
I confess this in the unattached dharmata of nonarising.

Not understanding that samsara is devoid of a self-nature,
One apprehends concrete and attributed phenomena to
 be permanent
And fixates on attributes out of unvirtuous karma.
I openly confess this in the space of faultless
 enlightenment.

When not realizing the equal nature as being equality,
One apprehends friends and deluded companions to be
  permanent.
How mistaken is this mind of an ignorant person.
I openly confess this in the space of the nature of
  equality.

When not facing the true nature of dharmata,
One abandons the true nature and endeavors in
  unvirtuous actions.
Discarding the Buddha's words, one is deceived by
  mundane distractions.
I openly confess this in the dharmata space of great bliss.

When awareness wisdom is not liberated in itself,
One abandons the self-cognizant nature and endeavors
  in distracted actions.
How pitiful is such a meaningless sentient being!
I openly confess this in the space free from approaching
  or keeping distance.

Wisdom deities and protectors possessing the samaya,
If this yogi who practices the samayas correctly
Happens to have the delusion of not realizing the view,
I openly confess it with deep remorse and regret.

This confession was extracted from *The Ocean of Amrita,*
a great accomplishment terma, practice text.

Yeshe Tsogyal

The Aspiration
of Yeshe Tsogyal

Guru Rinpoche
Revealed by Pema Ledrel Tsal

E ma ho
Through the merit we have accumulated in the three
    times,
May demons, obstacles, and opposing forces be pacified.
May we have long life without sickness, and
May we practice the Dharma in happiness and well-
    being.

By the power of practicing the Dharma with devotion,
May the teachings of the Buddha spread and flourish.
By establishing samsaric sentient beings in happiness,
May the wishes of the holy gurus be fulfilled.

Through the guru's kindness, may we,
All Dharma brothers and sisters,

Be free from the kleshas of anger and attachment.
Endowed with the splendor of the three vows of pure
discipline,

May we increase the qualities of experience and realization.
By the wisdom of realizing mahamudra,
May we benefit whomever we meet.
Together with all our followers,

May we enjoy unconditioned great bliss
And be guided to the Lotus-Arrayed Realm.
In that supreme and sacred blissful realm,
May we be one with the stainless, victorious body

Of the guru of the three kayas, Orgyen Padma,
And realize the dharmakaya that benefits us.
Through the compassion that benefits others,
Until samsara is emptied,

May we tame beings by teaching in whatever way is
necessary.
May we work for the benefit of all through rupakaya
manifestations.
May we accomplish the benefit of beings by stirring the
depths of samsara.
The three kayas inseparable, samsara and nirvana
totally freed,

Unfabricated, spontaneously present, luminous, and
  uncompounded,
The body of the vajra holder, changeless throughout the
  three times,
May this omniscient and complete enlightenment be
  swiftly attained.

This prayer, spoken by Yeshe Tsogyal, was taken from
The Khandro Nyingtig, The Heart Essence of the Dakinis.

BIOGRAPHICAL NOTES

CHOKGYUR LINGPA (1829–70) A treasure revealer and contemporary of Jamyang Khyentse Wangpo and Jamgon Kongtrul. He is regarded as one of the major tertons in Tibetan history, and his termas are widely practiced by both the Kagyü and Nyingma schools. For more details, see *The Life and Teachings of Chokgyur Lingpa* (Nepal: Rangjung Yeshe Publications, 1988).

DUDJOM LINGPA (1835–1904) A great adept and terton whose terma revelations fill twenty volumes. He was considered to be the emanation of Khye'u Chung Lotsawa, one of the twenty-five disciples of Guru Rinpoche. See *A Clear Mirror* (Nepal: Rangjung Yeshe Publications, 2011).

DUDJOM RINPOCHE (1904–87) The reincarnation of Dudjom Lingpa. He is regarded as one of the most prominent scholars and realized masters of our time.

GAMPOPA (1079–1153) The foremost disciple of Milarepa who possessed both supreme realization and great scholarship. He was the author of numerous texts including *The Jewel Ornament of Liberation*.

GURU RINPOCHE The lotus-born tantric master who, at the invitation of King Trisong Deutsen, established Vajrayana Buddhism in Tibet in the 9th century. He hid innumerable Dharma treasures throughout Tibet, Nepal, and Bhutan to be revealed by destined disciples in the centuries to come. He is also known by the names Padmasambhava and Padmakara.

JAMGON KONGTRUL (1813–99) A leader at the forefront of the nonsectarian *rimey* movement in the 19th century. Renowned as an accomplished master, scholar, and writer, he authored more than one hundred volumes of scripture. The most well-known are his *Five Treasuries,* and the sixty-three volumes of the *Rinchen Terdzo,* the collected terma literature of the one hundred great tertons. He is also known as Lodro Thaye and by his terton name Chimey Yungdrung Lingpa.

JAMYANG KHYENTSE WANGPO (1820–92) The last of the five great tertons, regarded as the combined reincarnation of Vimalamitra and King Trisong Deutsen. He became the master and teacher of all the Buddhist schools of Tibet and the founder of the nonsectarian *rimey* movement. In addition to his termas,he left ten volumes of works.

KARMAPA RANGJUNG DORJE (1284–1334) The third holder of the title *karmapa* and a great siddha, scholar, and propagator of both the mahamudra and dzogchen teachings to such an extent that he is also counted among the lineage gurus of the Nyingma tradition.

KHENPO GANGSHAR (20th century) One of the root gurus of both Chögyam Trungpa and Thrangu Rinpoche. In addition to being a learned scholar, he is known to have performed many deeds as a crazy yogi.

LONGCHENPA (1308–63) An incarnation of Princess Pema Sal, the daughter of King Trisong Deutsen, to whom Guru Rinpoche entrusted his own lineage of dzogchen known as *Khandro Nyingthig.* He is regarded as the most important writer on dzogchen teachings. His works include the *Seven Great Treasuries,* the *Three Trilogies,* and his commentaries in the *Nyingthig Yabshi.*

MILAREPA (1040–1123) One of the most famous yogis and poets in Tibetan religious history. Much of the teachings of the Kagyü schools passed through him.

MIPHAM RINPOCHE (1846–1912) A student of Jamgon Kongtrul, Jamyang Khyentse Wangpo, and Paltrul Rinpoche. Blessed by Manjushri, he became one of the greatest scholars of his time. His collected works fill more than thirty volumes. His chief disciple was Shechen Gyaltsab Pema Namgyal.

NAROPA. A great Indian *mahasiddha,* the chief disciple of Tilopa, and the guru of Marpa. See *The Life and Teachings of Naropa* (Boston: Shambhala, 1999) and *The Life of Marpa the Translator* (Boston: Shambhala, 1995).

Nyoshul Khen Rinpoche (1932–99) Regarded during his lifetime as the greatest living scholar of the Nyingma tradition. Renowned for his spontaneous poetry and songs of realization, he was one of the holders of the Nyingthig hearing lineage, which comes from Jigmey Lingpa and Paltrul Rinpoche.

Padmasambhava *See Guru Rinpoche.*

Pema Karpo (1527–1692) The Fourth Drukchen Rinpoche and head of the Drukpa Kagyü lineage,who was a master renowned for both his scholarshipand accomplishment.

Pema Ledrel Tsal (1291–1315?) The incarnation of the daughter of King Trisong Deutsen who revealed the dzogchen teachings of Guru Rinpoche known as *Khandro Nyingthig*. His following rebirth was Longchenpa.

Samantabhadra The primordially enlightened state of buddhahood from which all other buddhas of the peaceful and wrathful mandalas emanate. This buddha principle is the ultimate source of all the tantras.

Senge Wangchuk (11th–12th centuries) Chetsun Senge Wangchuk is counted among the lineage gurus in the Nyingthig transmission. As a result of his high level of realization, his physical body disappeared in rainbow light at the time of his death.

Shechen Gyaltsab Pema Namgyal (1871–1926) The chief disciple and lineage holder of Mipham Rinpoche. He was one of Dilgo Khyentse Rinpoche's root gurus.

Terdag Lingpa Gyurme Dorje (1646–1714) The builder of Mindrol Ling Monastery in Central Tibet, one of the most important Nyingma monasteries. He is especially remembered for this verse he uttered just before passing away.

Tilopa. A great Indian *mahasiddha* of the 10th and 11th centuries, the guru of Naropa, and the father of the Kagyü lineage.

Tsele Natsok Rangdrol (b. 1608) A reincarnation of the great Drukpa Kagyü master Götsangpa, himself considered to be an emanation of Milarepa. Jamyang Khyentse Chökyi Lodrö and Dilgo Khyentse Rinpoche both encouraged the study of his writings, as they are particularly suited to beings of these times.

TSOKDRUG RANGDROL (16th century) A Drukpa Kagyü master. The text includedhere was requested by Ngawang Kunga Tendzin who was the 3rd Khamtrul Rinpoche (1569–1637).

TULKU URGYEN RINPOCHE (1920–96) A holder of the Kagyü and Nyingma traditions who was among Tibetan Buddhism's greatest masters of the 20th century, and pivotal in bringing Dzogchen to the West.

VIMALAMITRA. Along with Guru Rinpoche and Vairotsana, one of the three main forefathers who established the dzogchen teachings, especially the instruction section, in Tibet in the 9th century. He is said to have attained rainbow body.

YESHE TSOGYAL (9th century) The chief Tibetan female disciple of Guru Rinpoche who received almost all the transmissions he passed on in Tibet and later compiled his teachings. After living for more than two hundred years, she went to the Copper-Colored Mountain without leaving any physical remains behind.

Glossary

BARDO. An intermediate state. The general teachings outline six bardos. Two of these, the bardo of meditation and the bardo of dreams, occur within the bardo of this life, which is defined as the period following birth until the onset of death. The process of passing away is called the bardo of dying. The bardo of dharmata occurs immediately after death, with the cessation of the outer and inner breath. Finally, the stage in which the consciousness seeks a new rebirth is called the bardo of becoming.

BODHICHITTA. See *bodhisattva*.

BODHISATTVA. Someone who has developed bodhichitta—the aspiration to attain enlightenment in order to benefit all sentient beings—and thus is a practitioner of the Mahayana path. The term is especially used to refer to noble bodhisattvas who have attained at least the first bhumi.

BUDDHAS OF THE FIVE FAMILIES. See *five female buddhas* and *five male buddhas*.

COMPLETION STAGE. One of the two aspects of Vajrayana practice. Completion stage with marks refers to yogic practices such as *tummo*. Completion stage without marks is the practice of dzogchen. See also *development and completion*.

DEMONS. The four maras. The first is the demon of the Lord of Death, which cuts our life short. Second is the demon of the physical aggregates, which prevents the attainment of the rainbow body. Third is the demon of the disturbing emotions, the three poisons that prevent liberation from samsara. Finally there is the demon of the child of the gods, which is procrastination and distraction.

The real demon is our conceptual thinking. By recognizing our mind-essence, all demons are defeated; the four maras are vanquished, and all obstacles are done away with.

DEVELOPMENT AND COMPLETION. The two main aspects, means and knowledge, of Vajrayana practice. *See also development stage and completion stage.*

DEVELOPMENT STAGE. One of the two aspects of Vajrayana practice. This involves the mental creation of pure images in order to purify habitual tendencies. The essence of the development stage is pure perception or sacred outlook, which means to perceive sights, sounds, and thoughts as deity, mantra, and wisdom, respectively.

DZOGCHEN. The highest teachings of the Early Translations Nyingma school, also known as the great perfection and atiyoga. Dzogchen teachings have two chief aspects: the lineage of scriptures and the lineage of teachings. The scriptures are contained in the tantras of the three sections of dzogchen: the mind section, space section, and instruction section. The lineage of teachings is embodied in the oral instructions one receives personally from a qualified master and holder of the dzogchen lineage.

ETERNALISM AND NIHILISM. The two poles of the spectrum of philosophical viewpoints. Eternalism is the belief that there is a permanent and causeless creator of everything, in particular, that one's identity or consciousness has a concrete essence that is independent, everlasting, and singular. Nihilism, in Tibetan, is literally "the view of discontinuance"—the extreme view of nothingness, namely that there is no such thing as rebirth or karmic effects and that the mind ceases to exist at death.

FIVE AGGREGATES. The five aspects that comprise the physical and mental constituents of a sentient being: physical forms, sensations, conceptions, formations, and consciousnesses.

FIVE ELEMENTS. Earth, water, fire, wind, and space.

FIVE FEMALE BUDDHAS. Dhatvishvari, Mamaki, Lochana, Pandaravasini, and Samayatara.

FIVE MALE BUDDHAS. Vairotsana, Akshobhya, Ratnasambhava, Amitabha, and Amoghasiddhi.

KARMA. The unerring law that virtuous actions yield virtuous results and that unvirtuous actions yield unvirtuous results. Specifically, it refers to the voluntary actions of thought, word, and deed, the effects of which determine the rebirths and experiences of individual sentient beings.

KNOWLEDGE. *See means and knowledge.*

KUSULU. A type of yogi, doing what comes naturally.

MADHYAMAKA. *See middle way.*

MAHAMUDRA. Literally, "the great seal," a very direct practice for realizing one's buddha nature. This system of teachings forms the basic view of Vajrayana practice according to the New Translations schools of the Kagyü, Gelug, and Sakya. In particular, the essential view of our natural state is introduced directly and without being dependent upon philosophical reasoning.

MARA. *See demons.*

MEANS AND KNOWLEDGE (PRAJNA AND UPAYA). The knowledge of realizing egolessness and the method or technique that brings about such realization.

MIDDLE WAY (MADHYAMAKA). The highest of the four Buddhist schools of philosophy. The middle way means not holding any extreme views, especially those of eternalism or nihilism.

MIND (SEM). The relative deluded mind that conceives the duality of self and other.

NIHILISM. *See eternalism and nihilism.*

PRAJNA. *See means and knowledge.*

PURE PERCEPTION. A special quality of Vajrayana practice, also known as sacred outlook, in which we practice seeing things as they actually are, not in the ordinary deluded way we think they are—for instance, that earth is simply solid matter, water is merely water, wind is wind, and so forth. In actuality, what appears to us as the ordinary experience of the five elements are the five female buddhas; the five aggregates are the five male buddhas, and so forth. Therefore, training oneself in pure perception is not a way of convincing oneself that things are what they are not, but rather it is training in seeing things as they truly are.

RAINBOW BODY. An occurrence at the death of a practitioner who has reached the exhaustion of all grasping and fixation through the dzogchen practice of togal, in which the elements of the physical body dissolve back into their essences of five-colored light, sometimes leaving behind only the hair and nails.

SIDDHIS, COMMON AND SUPREME. Accomplishment brought about through meditation practice. The supreme siddhi is the accomplishment of complete enlightenment. The common siddhis include eight types of miraculous powers, such as invisibility, fleetfootedness, and clairvoyance.

THREE CONCEPTS. The concepts of a subject, object, and action.

TERMA(TREASURE). Transmissions hidden, primarily by Guru Rinpoche and Yeshe Tsogyal, as texts or objects or teachings concealed in a disciple's mind, to be uncovered later by a treasure revealer for the benefit of future disciples.

TERTON (TREASURE REVEALER). A person chosen by Guru Rinpoche to reveal specific terma at a specific time. Such persons are usually incarnations of one of Guru Rinpoche's twenty-five close personal disciples.

TREASURE. *See terma.*

TREASURE REVEALER. *See terton.*

UPAYA. *See means and knowledge.*

VAJRAYANA. Literally, "Vajra Vehicle." This vehicle teaches the practices of taking the result as the path and is also known as Secret Mantra.